THE
POWER OF
EXPLICIT
TEACHING
AND DIRECT
INSTRUCTION

THE
POWER OF
EXPLICIT
TEACHING
AND DIRECT
INSTRUCTION

GREG ASHMAN

SAGE Publications Ltd
1 Oliver's Yard
55 City Road
London EC1Y 1SP

CORWIN
A SAGE company
2455 Teller Road
Thousand Oaks, California 91320
(0800)233-9936
www.corwin.com

SAGE Publications India Pvt Ltd
B 1/I 1 Mohan Cooperative Industrial Area
Mathura Road
New Delhi 110 044

SAGE Publications Asia-Pacific Pte Ltd
3 Church Street
#10-04 Samsung Hub
Singapore 049483

Editor: James Clark
Assistant Editor: Diana Alves
Senior project editor: Chris Marke
Marketing manager: Dilhara Attygalle
Cover design: Lisa Harper-Wells
Typeset by: C&M Digitals (P) Ltd, Chennai, India

Library of Congress Control Number: 2020940467

British Library Cataloguing in Publication data

A catalogue record for this book is available from the British Library

ISBN 978-1-5297-3161-3
ISBN 978-1-5297-3160-6 (pbk)

CONTENTS

ABOUT THE AUTHOR

 Greg Ashman grew up in the UK. In 1997, after studying Natural Sciences at Cambridge, he began training as a teacher at the Institute of Education in London. He went on to teach in three London comprehensive schools and took on roles including Head of Science, Assistant Headteacher and Deputy Headteacher. In 2010, he moved to Ballarat, Australia, with his young family. Since then, he has worked as Head of Mathematics at Ballarat Clarendon College. During this time, he has developed an interest in education research and is currently undertaking a PhD in Instructional Design, as well as taking on the role of Head of Research at Clarendon.

ACKNOWLEDGEMENTS

A lot of people have supported me and given me food for thought when writing this book. I would like to thank everyone involved in researchED and, in particular, its founder, Tom Bennett. I would like to thank the wider Twitter community of bloggers and researchers for their support and ideas, and acknowledge the wisdom to be found in Max Coltheart's Developmental Disorders of Language and Literacy Network. I would like to thank Mandy Nayton and Pim Pollen for giving me the opportunity to speak at extraordinary conferences and meet fascinating people.

I have only managed to scratch the surface of explicit teaching, but the picky-picky detail is to be found in the work of giants such as Siegfried Engelmann, Barak Rosenshine and Thomas Good, among others. Any mistakes or misunderstandings that remain in this book are entirely my own fault.

I want to pay tribute to the hard work of my colleagues and, in particular, Adelle Holmes, David Parker, Amber Ripley and Caiti Wade who have the misfortune to teach parallel classes to mine and who demonstrate unwavering patience as I try to learn as much as I can from them. I would like to thank David Shepherd, Jan McClure and the leadership of Ballarat Clarendon College, as well as all of the dedicated colleagues I work with.

Finally, a special mention must go to Jo, Rose and Catherine, my family. Their love, support and understanding were crucial in seeing this project through.

AUTHOR'S NOTE

In 2016, I self-published an ebook, *Ouroboros*. It was written over the summer and idiosyncratically and giddily careened through a few topics of particular interest to me at that time. These topics were loosely held together by the metaphor of the Ouroborous, a serpent or dragon that eats its own tail.

I am sure many who may otherwise have been tempted to take a look at *Ouroboros* never did so because they couldn't figure out what it was about. I am sure of this because a number of people told me so.

After the publication of my first book with SAGE Publishing, *The Truth About Teaching*, James Clark, my editor, and I discussed the idea of a second edition of *Ouroboros*, sharpening its agenda around the specific issue of explicit teaching. This book is the result of that discussion.

In the end, not much of *Ouroboros* remains. When you return to something you have written after four years, you tend to be able to think of different ways to explain things and of better evidence to draw upon – evidence that, in many cases, only accumulated in the intervening period. Those who are familiar with *Ouroboros* will sense its skeletal remains in Chapters 2, 3 and 4. The rest of the chapters are entirely new.

PREFACE

I took my first few steps into teaching in the summer of 1997. Since that time, I have learnt two important lessons. First, there is nothing wrong with explicitly teaching a knowledge-rich curriculum; second, improvements in education are usually the sum of many small parts.

I began as a guilty teacher. Through my training, I absorbed a view of education that I would not have been able to name at the time. Essentially, explaining concepts directly to students was a last resort – a sign of failure. Ideally, I should craft my lessons – I taught science back then – in such a way that students had a series of eureka moments when they figured out key concepts for themselves.

One exercise I completed as part of my training was to interview two 16-year-old students about how satellites orbit the Earth. As expected, they both told me that rockets push the satellites around. Gently, I probed the practicalities of this. Would the satellites not quickly run out of fuel? I now realise that this is an appalling way to try to teach students about satellite motion. Over the years, I have developed an explanation based on a thought experiment by Isaac Newton that I believe would allow most 11-year-olds to grasp the key idea behind satellites.

So, what was I doing back then? Mostly, I was feeling guilty. I was feeling guilty that I somehow couldn't get it to work the way it was supposed to. I would fall back on explaining things to students like a patrol under fire falling back to base. The problem was that my explanations were not as good as they could have been.

I now know there is a wealth of research on 'direct instruction' or 'explicit teaching'. Back then, I didn't even have a proper name for it. It was 'traditional', with all the baggage that entails, or it was 'chalk and talk'.

I now know that the evidence for explicit teaching is strong. It is not inferior to asking students to figure things out for themselves – quite the reverse. I also know what highly effective forms of explicit teaching look like and they don't look like the forms I used to retreat into as a young teacher. I could have been so much better if I had known then what I know now.

In my current role, I often interview new teachers who have just completed teacher education courses at university, and their experience is similar to mine all those years ago. They just don't know much about explicit teaching. It is interesting to ponder why. There are many reasons, but one that I believe is often overlooked is that explicit teaching lives in the details and details are not sexy. Once you take responsibility for fully communicating complex concepts, rather than somehow infusing them incidentally into students' minds, it becomes a series of technical challenges. What is the best way of presenting a fraction? How can we communicate Lenz's law to avoid a common misconception? Exactly what do students need to know in order to discuss Truman's decision to use atomic weapons against Japan?

When you involve yourself, as I have, in the detail of improving a department curriculum over a span of five or more years, you begin to realise that improvement is the sum of many tiny parts. There is no single big thing that you can put in place and then quickly reap the benefits. And that's not sexy.

Advocate as I am for explicit teaching, I am happy to admit that if trainee teachers had a better understanding of the research, it would not revolutionise teaching overnight. Experienced teachers using a well-planned enquiry learning curriculum, iterated over a number of years, will be more effective than a novice who knows about Rosenshine. There are no quick fixes here.

What I offer instead is a better, fuller understanding – an inching closer to the truth about education. I offer it as the foundation you probably never had. I offer it as a shorter, straighter route to the effectiveness that experience brings. I offer it as the missing part of the puzzle.

Now, if you'll let me explain . . .

1

ON THE SHOULDERS OF GIANTS

Key Points

- Academic education is not a natural process and there is no reason to think that the way we learn to talk is the best way to learn academic content.
- Before we decide how to teach, we have to decide what to teach, although these two questions are linked.
- Explicit teaching is effective for teaching a body of knowledge.
- A knowledge-rich curriculum is superior to one based on ill-defined skills or student interest.

In a letter to Robert Hooke in 1676, Isaac Newton wrote: 'If I have seen further it is by standing on ye sholders of Giants.' Newton was alluding to those who had come before, such as Galileo Galilei, on whose work he had built. The metaphor, implying the ratchet-like progress of human understanding, privileging accumulated culture over the gifted and inspired individual, was not original. A little research establishes an earlier form attributed to Bernard of Chartres by John of Salisbury. Given the nature of the saying, its history is satisfying. Or it should be. The stuff of teaching is to pass on accumulated culture so that our children and their children may see further than we ever did. And yet the forces ranged against such a simple and obvious proposition, as intelligible to Newton as it is to us today, are formidable.

There are those who see education as a development from within. Kieran Egan charts the historical influence of this idea in *Getting it Wrong from the Beginning* (Egan, 2004). Nineteenth- and early twentieth-century 'progressivist' philosophers of education, such as Herbert Spencer, mixed older, romantic ideas about childhood and nature with a form of pseudoscience inspired by the recently developed theory of evolution to claim that the development of individual children recapitulates the evolutionary ascent of humanity as a species. The educator's role was to get out of the way of this natural process. Instead of placing children on the shoulders of giants, we should place them in a woodland glade to play, discover and learn.

If children are to develop naturally through experience, there is little need to directly teach them boring facts about the past in an artificial environment such as a classroom. Instead, the educator's role, if any, is to manipulate the environment in order to ensure that the child's experiences are rich enough. Although on initial inspection it may seem absurd, such ideas have gained considerable purchase in the education world, particularly on those rarefied mountain tops least concerned with practicalities – the education conference circuit, the column inches produced by broadsheet pundits and the education faculties of our universities.

Lighting a fire

I qualified to teach by completing a Postgraduate Certificate of Education (PGCE) at the Institute of Education in London. Early in the course, a lecturer referred to a famous quote from Plutarch, a quote that is often misattributed to Socrates or even W.B. Yeats. The sense in which the quote was used was to suggest that children are not 'empty vessels' into which teachers must pour knowledge. Instead, we must light a fire inside them – an inspiring idea.

I accepted this message and carried it with me for a long time. It sounded profound and I understood it to represent a significant psychological truth. I trusted my lecturers. I trusted that they understood the research. I felt guilty about using explicit approaches to teaching because I didn't think they were supported by the evidence.

Years later, I decided to investigate the Plutarch quote for myself. His advice is not for teachers (Plutarch, 1927). He is advising a young man, Nicander, on how he should *listen* to lectures: don't just bask in the glow of a warm, erudite lecture; mull over the concepts and take something away with you; make it your own.

If anyone is unsure about the role that Plutarch perceives for students, then a different quote from the same text clarifies the matter:

> As skilful horse-trainers give us horses with a good mouth for the bit, so too skilful educators give us children with a good ear for speech, by teaching them to hear much and speak little. (Plutarch, 1927)

For some reason, my lecturer had left that part out.

Constructivism

The textbooks I was assigned at university had a focus on students' misconceptions. They described the thinking of Piaget, Vygotsky and Bruner, and a theory known as 'constructivism'. I now realise that constructivism played a dominant role in framing the training I received.

The theory of constructivism posited that:

> The teacher's role is to facilitate learning. For pupils simply to acquire a body of knowledge or set of facts is not a constructive approach or adequate achievement for the pupil. The teacher must set the classroom in a way that allows pupils to enquire, by posing problems, creating a responsive environment and

> giving assistance to the pupils to achieve autonomous discoveries. This applies to all areas of education, from discovering prose and its meaning in English to design problems in technology. (Capel et al., 1996)

This description of constructivism will annoy some readers who will insist that it is not a theory of how to teach, but instead is a theory of learning. Adding further confusion, there are a number of related constructivist theories such as social constructivism and radical constructivism that vary in key ways. Perhaps of most interest to cognitive scientists is cognitive constructivism and a view that the mind consists of mental 'schemas' that new learning has to interact with, either to fit in to a current schema or to change it (Derry, 1996). If true, constructivism describes the way that people learn whether they are independently discovering concepts or listening to lectures.

I am sympathetic to this view of constructivism as a theory of learning, but I must insist, in turn, that this is not the view of many protagonists who clearly see the theory as having implications for the way we teach. Plucked from its philosophical and scientific roots, constructivism in the classroom usually equates to asking students to find something out for themselves – to 'construct' knowledge rather than passively receive it like empty vessels. Perhaps it is the case that an older idea has found a new, more scientific tone of expression.

It is as if the giant is there, offering children his shoulders, but instead we are asking them to construct a ladder out of sticky tape and drinking straws.

As is often the case, we can find a prototypical version of constructivism in the writings of John Dewey, way back in his 1916 work, *Democracy and Education*:

> Why is it, in spite of the fact that teaching by pouring in, learning by a passive absorption, are universally condemned, that they are still so entrenched in practice? That education is not an affair of 'telling' and being told, but an active and constructive process, is a principle almost as generally violated in practice as conceded in theory. Is not this deplorable situation due to the fact that the doctrine is itself merely told?

However, anyone so bold as to interpret Dewey in this way is likely to be told they have misunderstood him.

Knowledge or experience?

So far, I have conflated two distinct concepts. The first is that there is a body of knowledge that is worth teaching – i.e. that it is worth standing on the giant's shoulders – and the second is the concept of directly teaching this knowledge, the main subject of this book. In theory, these are separable. We could, for instance, insist that there is a body of knowledge worth teaching, but that the best way to teach it is to place students in carefully crafted situations where we ensure that they discover this key knowledge for themselves. Alternatively, we could insist that there is no specific body of knowledge worth passing on to students, but that teachers should still be involved in the process of direct teaching, perhaps by teaching general-purpose skills instead. Both of these approaches have currency. We could argue that some forms of science teaching are examples of the former, and perhaps the teaching of reading comprehension strategies is an example of the latter.

However, as I will go on to argue, explicit teaching is particularly effective at transmitting knowledge from one person to another. This tends to lead to two general gravitational influences that are hard to avoid. Those who want students to gain a specific body of knowledge tend to be drawn, inevitably if sometimes slowly, to explicit forms of teaching. Those who dislike direct teaching in favour of more experiential approaches tend to find themselves arguing that transmitting a body of knowledge is not, and never has been, the point of education; that it is more about the acquisition of *experiences* that shape the character or, in its more modern variation, develop various generic skills such as critical thinking (see, for example, Macfarlane, 2020). It is not about standing on the giant's shoulders, but the experience of acting like a giant and thinking like a giant.

This is not a new idea. Writing about the curriculum in 1918, Franklin Bobbit advocated a play-based approach to the formative years of schooling and advised:

> There is not to be too much *teaching*. What the children crave and need is *experience*. The school's main task is to supply opportunities so varied and attractive that, like the two boys when they arrived at port, pupils want to plunge in and to enjoy the opportunities that are placed before them. (Bobbit, 1918)

It is hard to hold on to the idea of passing on a specific body of knowledge while also committing to following the contours of children's varying interests and the experiences that may be devised in pursuit of them, although Bobbitt insists that his approach lays the 'solid foundations for the later industrial studies'.

Unnatural

Nevertheless, an emphasis on play, especially in the first few years of formal education, is understandable. Children learn a great deal of things through play, such as the rules of games and the attendant social skills to navigate them. Notably, most children learn to speak their native language with very little explicit teaching apart from the occasional correction such as, 'It's *brought* not *bringed*'. You do not need schools for this.

So, from the perspective of an early twentieth-century reformer, surveying the landscape of little school houses with their recitation, slates and harsh discipline, an obvious reform would be to make learning more joyous and playful. Perhaps nature was showing us the way and our factory-farmed industrial mindset was refusing to see it. Children need to graze in green pastures, yet we were cramming them in to feed lots.

There is, however, a fundamental difference between learning to understand someone who is *speaking* your native language and learning to *read* it. For most of humanity's time on Earth, writing has not existed. Its origins span a few millennia. Even then, for much of those few millennia, its secrets were held by the priestly, clerical and elite of society. Mass literacy is less than a couple of centuries old in industrialised societies and even more recent elsewhere.

Yet, since the deep, unrecorded past, we have been speaking and listening to each other. It is hard to know exactly when speech arose or reached its current level of sophistication because spoken words leave no fossils, but it is reasonable to assume that it has been subject to the process of evolution. According to David Geary (1995), an evolutionary psychologist, this could represent a key distinction. There are some bodies of knowledge and skills that we have evolved to learn, with play and experience being the ways we have evolved to learn them. In contrast, there are more recent products of human culture that we have not had time to evolve to learn. If Geary is right, play may not necessarily be the best way to learn these more recently created bodies of knowledge and skills. This frees us to seek evidence for the best way to learn them, and we will see that the evidence points towards explicit teaching.

If I learn this, will I be able to buy a Mercedes?

Before we set out to teach in the most effective way possible, it is important to decide *what* to teach. What are the products of more recent human culture that are worth learning? This question must be answered, to a greater or lesser extent, by all who would design a school curriculum.

There are a number of principles we may keep in mind. We may take a functional view – what knowledge will students *need* in the future? What will they need for the work they will do? The trouble with a question like this is that it dissolves the more you look at it. On one level, you can continue to exist without most of the things we learn in school. You can even be highly successful. Jeremy Clarkson, a prominent reviewer of cars, has a habit of appearing every year on the day that 18-year-olds in England receive the results of national exams, pointing out that he failed his exams and noting that he is nevertheless capable of affording the tasteless trappings of conspicuous wealth (Mylrea, 2017).

Another approach is to ask essentially the same question but frame it probabilistically: What is *likely* to be *most* useful in the future? This is the point at which a small army of commentators reach for their crystal balls and make confident predictions about the unknowable: there will be a rise in the use of artificial intelligence or robots or self-propelled dirigibles (I made up that one) that will lead to an increase or maybe a decrease in manufacturing. What is certain is that students will not need to know facts any longer because machines can do that for them. Instead, they will need to develop the uniquely human qualities that machines cannot emulate and, by a remarkable coincidence, this will require the kind of education advocated for by nineteenth-century progressivists, along with perhaps some computer programming (see, for example, Monbiot, 2017; Benn, 2020).

I find this unconvincing. The only certainty about the future is its unpredictability. When I was at secondary school in the late 1980s and early 1990s, I remember being instructed in how to use the word-processing software packages *Edword* and *View* on a mouse-less BBC microcomputer. During one lesson, we were taught the commands required to justify text in *View*. No doubt, the thinking behind this lesson was that it would be functionally useful – that it would in some way prepare us for the future. It did not, of course. That knowledge was ephemeral, obsolescent. Nevertheless, the linear equations, the history of the Industrial Revolution and the German for 'What did you do at the weekend?' that I learnt are as valid today as they were then.

This illustrates a key principle for curriculum design. Concepts do not have a fixed lifespan. Some concepts are more enduring than others because they have more value. How, then, are we to pick the more valuable ones – the ones that are likely to persist in being valuable long into the future? One indication is that they have already endured, that these concepts have survived change in the past. If we have found a cultural artefact to be valuable for fifty, a hundred or maybe a thousand years, then it is certainly possible that it will be rendered obsolete by impending technological or societal change. However, this seems less likely than for a concept that has been around for just a few months or years. Although possible, I doubt that linear equations will become obsolete any time soon, or that the Industrial Revolution will cease to have happened or have been important, or that people in Germany will stop asking each other what they did at the weekend or alter the language they use to do this.

Reading for meaning

Perhaps of all the enduringly useful things to know, the ability to read sits at the apex. Those who disagree on pretty much all other educational issues are likely to value literacy, even if the term has been rendered ambiguous by a tendency to encompass ever more concepts that are unrelated or only loosely related to reading and writing (see, for example, Perry, 2020).

Reading is important because it represents a doorway into the library of academic knowledge. If you cannot read, you cannot enter. The debate on reading instruction often focuses on the best method for teaching early reading – how to lift the squiggles off a page and turn them into words familiar from oral vocabulary. And yet there is a second element that is equally important (Gough and Tunmer, 1986; Nation, 2019). It is possible to be able to decode all the words in this way but still not understand the meaning of a text. It is like listening to a speaker, knowing all or most of the words the speaker is saying, but not being able to follow the argument. This is the problem of reading comprehension.

To illustrate this problem, consider the following text from a news report about the sport of cricket (Shemilt, 2015):

> Australia failed to fully capitalise on the second-wicket stand of 182 between Smith and Finch, as Michael Clarke's men were stunted by the off-breaks of Ravichandran Ashwin and a curious collective failure against back-of-a-length bowling.

If you follow cricket, then you will understand the text. However, if you do not, then you may experience the strange sensation of knowing all the words but still finding the text extremely hard to understand. Your knowledge of the words 'back', 'of', 'a', 'length' and 'bowling' will not help you picture what 'back-of-a-length bowling' is all about. Clearly, the issue here is a lack of knowledge of cricket, which is preventing comprehension.

Sport is good for illustrating this problem because it is a domain in which educated people often lack certain knowledge. When we know more about a particular domain, it may be harder to empathise with someone else's missing knowledge. Take an example from a news item that appeared on the BBC website (Kim Jong-un appears in public, 2020):

> Kim Jong-un has appeared in public for the first time in 20 days, North Korean state media says . . . . KCNA news agency reports that the North Korean leader cut the ribbon at the opening of a fertiliser factory.

An educated reader brings a lot to bear on an article such as this. There is an understanding of the political situation in North Korea and why it is significant that the report comes from the 'state media'. But there are also more subtle understandings such as what 'cut the ribbon' means. Functionally, this is similar to 'back-of-a-length bowling'.

A reader who does not understand this term may snag their attention on it, like a garment on a protruding nail, and fail to comprehend the sentence as a result.

Consider the kind of comprehension question we might ask a student about a passage like this: 'What is the main idea?' How many will think it is that Kim Jong-un opened a fertiliser factory?

E.D. Hirsch Jr has written extensively on how a lack of background knowledge leads to poor reading comprehension and how it is often the disadvantaged who suffer most from this knowledge gap (e.g. Hirsch, 2003, 2019). If we want young people to be able to engage with sources of news, such as the *BBC News* website, so that they may better use their voice and shape the world of the future, they need a broad knowledge base. This does not necessarily mean directly teaching them facts about North Korea and every other possible newsworthy issue, but it would certainly entail placing them in that virtuous circle where sufficient knowledge provides access to more knowledge and an ever-accumulating understanding of the world.

Because a curriculum of function – of *need* – is a lowly ambition, we should be seeking a curriculum of human flourishing. Nobody *needs* to attend their local theatre to enjoy a Shakespeare play, but if we do not teach the knowledge that is sufficient to do so, we remove that particular possibility for leisure. Of course, many will choose a different leisure. That is fine. The job of teachers is to open up a world of potential and possibility. It is for young people themselves to chart their way through it.

The skill of using a search engine

Who, then, could be opposed to clearly defining a body of the most valuable knowledge that is worth teaching students? Lots of people, it seems. There are three main arguments that are deployed against a well-defined, knowledge-rich curriculum and they sometimes overlap.

The first is perhaps best expressed by Howard Gardner (2012), a developmental psychologist at Harvard Graduate School of Education:

> when the answers to factual questions are available at the movement of a mouse or the click of a button, there is no point in spending time committing the information to memory . . . going

forward, our focus in schools . . . should be on understanding the METHODS whereby assertions are made, the way that a question is posed, how relevant data and arguments are marshaled, what kinds of challenges have been considered, how have they been responded to, etc.

Gardner is expressing a commonplace observation: if any knowledge we may need is available on the internet, why do we want students to commit it to memory? Can they not just look it up when they need it? Instead, perhaps we should be teaching students to better evaluate knowledge when they look it up – a general-purpose skill. We need to get children thinking like a giant.

First, this argument raises the question as to why this has become so significant an issue *now*. The internet is a vast repository of information, but most of that information consists of the strings of zeros and ones coding for pictures of someone's lunch or a video clip of a cat flushing a toilet. The knowledge relevant to a school education and that is available on the Web is finite. It could be captured, more or less, in the books of a well-stocked library and it certainly has been captured in this way in the past. Why, then, did the advent of municipal libraries not negate the need for factual learning, at least in those who have had ongoing access to them? If now, then why not then?

The answer perhaps lies in two assumptions that are embedded in Gardner's argument. The first is that knowledge available at the 'click of a button' is qualitatively the same as knowledge available in the mind. This seems unlikely. We know how knowledge is encoded on the internet, but we do not know how it is encoded in the mind, or even if 'encoded' is the right word to use when discussing the mind. There is also a difference in the time it takes to retrieve knowledge from these different sources. However quickly you are able to click a button, read and comprehend the result, it will be many orders of magnitude slower than bringing much of the knowledge you possess into your conscious mind, with the latter often achieved with no conscious effort at all. Then there is the issue of interpreting external knowledge – fitting the square peg of what you find into the round hole of your perception – whereas the knowledge you already possess already fits.

As I mentioned above, at school, I studied the German language. As a young adult, I saw a copy of a German translation of *The Time Machine* by H.G. Wells in a second-hand bookshop. I bought it with the intention of reading it and looking up any words I did not understand in the German–English dictionary I had held on to from my school days.

At home, I placed the book and dictionary on my desk. I looked up the first word, then the second, then the third. Each verb and noun had several potential meanings. I couldn't quite see how they fitted together. I looked up another word. This did not feel like reading. This was not pleasurable. I gave up. I never reached comprehension.

The second assumption embedded in Gardner's argument is that, rather than knowledge, we can teach students some other sort of thing. Rather than memorising facts, students should be focusing on how assertions are made and questions are posed. This separates these ideas from their knowledge substrate and examines them independently. It implies they are something other than knowledge and, as such, are more powerful because they are not locked to some arbitrary context. Assertions are made and questions are posed in all fields of human understanding, so learning *how* they are made is far more useful than knowing the chemical formula of ethene. As we skip through the hyperlinks from one topic to another, we can apply these powerful understandings to whatever we find.

Interestingly, Gardner is probably best known for his controversial theory of multiple intelligences. This theory suggests that instead of one overall form of intelligence, individuals have a number of different forms of intelligence specific to different attributes, such as musical or interpersonal intelligence. Critics argue that the theory lacks empirical evidence (Waterhouse, 2006; Gardner and Moran, 2006) and even Gardner concedes that the theory has sometimes been misapplied in education (Gardner, 1995). Yet whether intelligence is multiple or not, this raises the question of what intelligence *is* and how it operates independently of knowledge. If we are using our intelligence(s) to understand how assertions are made or questions are posed then what exactly are we doing?

Perhaps Gardner's argument relies on a false dualism between knowledge and the mind – a false choice. What is a mind without knowledge? How do you think about something you do not know? Rather than seeing the mind as a set of library shelves and knowledge as the neatly ordered books that fill those shelves, perhaps we should see the mind as a set of tools *made out of* knowledge. Knowledge is what you think *with*. Knowledge *is* the mind.

Perhaps an understanding of the methods whereby questions are posed in, say, organic chemistry is a thing or set of things to be *known* in the field of organic chemistry, just like the chemical formula of ethene. It may be a slightly more general-purpose thing to know, but it will not necessarily help you understand how questions are posed in fine art criticism, with the latter being a thing or set of things to be known within the field of fine art criticism.

If these things to be known exist as assemblages in the mind – schemas – that are organised in terms of meaning and interrelatedness, then what we have, schematically, is a network of nodes. Yet it has a fractal nature. We may zoom in or out and see different relationships and different nodes encapsulating those relationships. Some overarch and encapsulate others. What we do not necessarily see is a difference in their nature. It's knowledge all the way up and its knowledge all the way down.

Dead, white, European men

Whose knowledge is the question at the heart of the second main objection to a clearly defined curriculum. When presented with the question of curriculum design, we are presented with the problem of prospectively deciding what knowledge we would like young people to have. That is a powerful role to assume and a potentially diabolical one. At one extreme we could, if we wished, attempt to teach false histories. Even if this is not our conscious plan, we may do so unintentionally because the bodies of knowledge we hold as a culture are imperfect and open to revision. Cultures evolve and perceptions change.

As I write, I am reflecting on an incident over the last few days in which Ben Newmark, a history teacher from the UK, posted on Twitter his plan for teaching an aspect of the history of the American West. The way in which Newmark had framed this issue triggered a public shaming event (Ronson, 2015) where large numbers of people on Twitter directed their anger towards him (Newmark, 2020). And yet it appears that the particular framing Newmark had used was required by the authority in England that sets the relevant history examination (Fordham, 2020). How can we resolve these kinds of issues while still maintaining a detailed curriculum?

Anyone who reflects on the cultural history of countries such as the United States, the United Kingdom and Australia will rub up against the problem of an overabundance of dead white men. Historically, a privileged class of European men dominate the literary, artistic and scientific canon. These are the giants on whose shoulders we are thinking about placing our young people. Yet what does this say to young people from different ethnic backgrounds? What does this say to young women?

Some of this imbalance is no doubt the result of chauvinism – a lingering lack of recognition of the fruits of other cultures or of their appropriation. Some may be due to historical accident. Should we redress this? How could we redress this? Should we actively seek works from a diverse range of cultures in order to show all are valued?

These are essentially political questions. What is the value embodied by the works of Newton, Shakespeare, Da Vinci? What is the value in knowing the history of a country's kings and queens? How are these to be balanced with calls for more diversity? Where should the balance fall? We are weighing apples against oranges and everyone will have a different opinion.

It is this quality that makes a question political, not the matter of who specifically is addressing the question. If a messy and heated argument takes place about the content of the curriculum among elected representatives, it is a political question. If it is decided by bureaucrats in a state education department or at an examination authority, it remains a political question. If it is decided by individual teachers after they close the classroom door, it is *still* a political question. I would rather have the public debate where everyone has their say and nobody gets everything they want than the radical deregulation of curriculum that characterises much of our education system today.

It is entirely understandable why politicians would prefer to focus on 'literacy' and 'numeracy' and supposedly general-purpose skills such as 'critical thinking'. Stripped of all specifics, these nouns offend nobody and being in the middle of the heat and fury of a culture war is unpleasant and distracting. But *someone* is still making those decisions.

Boring lessons

The third and final objection to a defined, knowledge-rich curriculum overlaps considerably with the second: by deciding the content of the curriculum for students, we remove the possibility for it to follow their interests. It is demotivating.

This may be because we have excluded aspects of our students' cultures or have failed to reflect the diversity of our students in the curriculum. However, it may simply be that some students find aspects of the curriculum just plain boring. Why require them to memorise facts about the water cycle and erosion if they have no interest in the subject and can see no relevance to their own lives? Instead, we need to cast aside a pre-prepared curriculum, or at least strip it back to a smaller set of essentials, in order to create the room to prioritise student choice and the relevance of the curriculum to students' lives.

Implicit in such arguments is a theory of motivation that may be formulated something like this: motivation is the starting point of learning. First, you must motivate students and then they will learn. One way to motivate them is to ensure that the content is relevant to their everyday lives.

David Perkins makes the case for stripping back the curriculum and prioritising relevance in his 2014 book, *Future Wise: Educating our Children for a Changing World*. Seemingly aware of the problem with focusing a curriculum only on the strictly functional, he introduces the concept of 'lifeworthy'. If an item is lifeworthy, then it is fit for inclusion in the curriculum. In my view, this leads to Perkins applying different measures to different curriculum items in a pretty arbitrary way. Quadratic equations should be removed for functional reasons – hardly anyone needs to use them. However, the French Revolution should be included, not because it has a functional value, but because of the important ideas it embodies and represents. This leads to something of an idiosyncratic list.

Perkins inadvertently highlights the flaw in the idea that relevance is (always) motivating when one proposal he makes for a maths activity is to ask students to plan, 'for their town's future water needs or model its traffic flow'. I have met many teenagers and they don't tend to be particularly excited by water management and urban planning. When faced with a choice between the mundane and escapism, they tend to prefer the latter. So real-world contexts are not the motivational winner we sometimes unthinkingly assume them to be.

And real-world contexts present us with a couple of additional problems. One consideration is their often complicated and messy nature. They may provide novice learners with too many things to pay attention to at once, some of which are not relevant to solving a particular problem or creating a particular solution, but that nonetheless have to be assessed as not relevant. This could potentially cause frustration and confusion, and this is one reason why some advocate breaking content down into small components for novices as an aid to motivation (Martin, 2016). Breaking something down into smaller components is a key strategy of explicit teaching, so again we see that although technically separate concepts, the *how* and the *what* of teaching do tend to have implications for each other.

The other, perhaps less obvious, problem arises when using familiar everyday contexts to teach abstract and counterintuitive concepts such as those found in the sciences. We already have mental schemas in place for these concepts, which are often incorrect from a scientific standpoint. For instance, a common misconception is that a force is required to make an object move. Newton's laws of motion instead state that a force is required to *change* the way an object is moving. Learning physics therefore requires a student to move from one conception of the world to another – a non-monotonic change. We may imagine that this involves reshaping the schemas involved, deleting and replacing nodes and links. Indeed, constructivists have often advocated for teachers to introduce 'cognitive conflict' where students are presented with observations that falsify pre-existing ideas as a way of forcing them make this conceptual change (Limón, 2001). However, evidence for the effectiveness of cognitive conflict is mixed (Ramsburg and Ohlsson, 2016) and we can point to real-world examples of people who, when proven irrefutably wrong, take the new information and still manage to reconcile it to their prior belief system. In 1956, Leon Festinger, Henry Riecken and Stanley Schachter released their influential study of a UFO-based religion whose adherents sold their possessions and readied themselves for the ending of the world at midnight on 21 December 1954. When the end of the world failed to materialise, they decided their religious activity must have saved it. Festinger went on to develop his theory of cognitive dissonance.

How may we explain these findings? Stellan Ohlsson (2009), a professor of psychology and computer science, has argued that the mind has no requirement to be internally consistent and individuals hedge their bets, able to hold on to to contradictory sets of ideas simultaneously as competing 'theories'. Successful non-monotonic change occurs when a new theory, such as Newton's laws of motion, outcompetes an old one by proving more useful, at least in particular sets of circumstances. If true, not only does this provide an interesting insight into human inconsistency, it implies that newly forming theories are best incubated away from the context in which the old conceptions are embedded, for fear that any new knowledge may be incorporated erroneously under the old theory. For instance, a student confronted with the fact that a football moving through the air has no apparent force acting to push it along may conclude that there must be an invisible force responsible for its motion, whereas the same student may be more prepared to accept the absence of a propelling force in a context that is abstract or unfamiliar, such as a computer simulation.

So, if real-world contexts are not a panacea for motivation and introduce some additional problems of their own, what is the solution for motivating students? When you begin to examine the literature on motivation, you realise it is one of education's more eel-like concepts and that it is hard to nail down. Instead, researchers tend to break it up into a number of different components. There are forms of interest such as situational and personal interest (Hidi, 2001). As the names imply, situational interest is interest in a particular event or episode, whereas personal interest is a more ongoing interest in a domain. To illustrate the difference, a science teacher exploding a balloon full of hydrogen may engender intense situational interest in a student, but that student may not go on to maintain a personal interest in science. Conversely, a student with a personal interest in science may maintain this interest through an activity, such as reading from a textbook, that may not cause situational interest in others. Other relevant constructs include students' perceptions of themselves – self-concept – and their perceptions of their own capabilities – self-efficacy (Bong and Clarke, 1999).

One aspect of motivation that is perhaps not as widely appreciated as it should be is the longitudinal relationship between measures that have been developed to assess motivation and academic achievement. There is at least a two-way effect – academic achievement leads to later motivation and vice versa (e.g. Pekrun et al., 2017) – and in some studies we even see that academic achievement leads to later motivation but that the reverse effect is notably absent (Garon-Carrier et al., 2015).

Self-determination theory is a psychological theory that suggests three basic needs affect the strength and type of motivation. Competence is one of these needs alongside autonomy and relatedness (Deci and Ryan, 2008). A recent study of over 30,000 college students found support for the predictions of self-determination theory but, of the three proposed needs, the need for competence predominated in its effect (Yu and Levesque-Bristol, 2020). So, various attempts to address the question of motivation seem to point in roughly the same direction.

In selecting a challenging academic topic, we may not generate immediate situational interest. However, through achievement in this area, a student may develop motivation *as a result*. Yet, an approach to curriculum that asks as its starting point, 'What are the most motivating contexts for learning?' seems misconceived. At best, these contexts will generate situational interest that may or may not lead to personal interest. What is absent is any appreciation of the ongoing motivational role of academic achievement.

Perhaps the twin goals of effective teaching and motivation are aligned. If so, we need to examine what effective teaching looks like.

References

BBC News (2020, 2 May) Kim Jong-un appears in public. North Korean state media report Retrieved from: www.bbc.com/news/world-asia-52508437

Benn, M. (2020, 1 May) This curious revolution avoids conflict and sidesteps inequality. *Schools Week*. Retrieved from: https://schoolsweek.co.uk/this-curious-revolution-avoids-conflict-and-sidesteps-inequality/

Bobbitt, J. (1918) *The Curriculum*. Boston, MA: Houghton Mifflin.

Bong, M. and Clark, R.E. (1999) Comparison between self-concept and self-efficacy in academic motivation research. *Educational Psychologist*, 34(3): 139–53. doi.10.1207/s15326985ep3403_1

Capel, S., Leask, M. and Turner, T. (1996) *Learning to Teach in the Secondary School: A Companion to School Experience*. London: Routledge.

Deci, E.L. and Ryan, R.M. (2008) Self-determination theory: A macrotheory of human motivation, development, and health. *Canadian Psychology/ Psychologie canadienne*, 49(3): 182.

Derry, S.J. (1996) Cognitive schema theory in the constructivist debate. *Educational Psychologist*, 31(3–4): 163–74.

Dewey, J. (1916) *Democracy and Education*. Project Gutenberg. Retrieved from: www.gutenberg.org/files/852/852-h/852-h.htm

Egan, K. (2004) *Getting it Wrong from the Beginning: Our Progressivist Inheritance from Herbert Spencer, John Dewey, and Jean Piaget*. New Haven, CT: Yale University Press.

Festinger, L., Riecken, H. and Schachter, S. (2017) *When Prophecy Fails: A Social and Psychological Study of a Modern Group that Predicted the Destruction of the World*. Morrisville, NC: Lulu Press.

Fordham, M. (2020, 30 April) Re American West: There are major issues in how it's taught in England. (Tweet). Retrieved from: https://twitter.com/mfordhamhistory/status/1255549518185213957

Gardner, H. (1995) Reflections on multiple intelligences: Myths and messages. *Phi Delta Kappan*, 77: 200.

Gardner, H. (2012, 26 April) *Educating for Innovative Societies*. (C. Davis, interviewer). Retrieved from: https://oecdedutoday.com/educating-for-innovative-societies/

Gardner, H. and Moran, S. (2006) The science of multiple intelligences theory: A response to Lynn Waterhouse. *Educational Psychologist*, 41(4): 227–32.

Garon-Carrier, G., Boivin, M., Guay, F., Kovas, Y., Dionne, G., Lemelin, J.-P., Séguin, J. R., Vitaro, F. and Tremblay, R. E. (2015) Intrinsic motivation and achievement in mathematics in elementary school: A longitudinal investigation of their association. *Child Development*, 87(1): 165–75.

Geary, D.C. (1995) Reflections of evolution and culture in children's cognition: Implications for mathematical development and instruction. *American Psychologist*, 50(1): 24.

Gough, P.B. and Tunmer, W.E. (1986) Decoding, reading, and reading disability. *Remedial and Special Education*, 7(1): 6–10.

Hidi, S. (2001) Interest, Psychology of. *International Encyclopedia of the Social & Behavioral Sciences*, 7712–15. https://doi.org/10.1016/b0-08-043076-7/01535-7

Hirsch, E.D. (2003) Reading comprehension requires knowledge of words and the world. *American Educator*, 27(1): 10–13.

Hirsch, E.D. (2019) *Why Knowledge Matters: Rescuing our Children from Failed Educational theories*. Cambridge, MA: Harvard Education Press.

Limón, M. (2001) On the cognitive conflict as an instructional strategy for conceptual change: A critical appraisal. *Learning and Instruction*, 11(4–5): 357–80.

Macfarlane, R. (2020, 29 April) Knowledge is not enough, growing effective learners must become our aim. *Big Education*. Retrieved from https://bigeducation.org/lfl-content/knowledge-is-not-enough-growing-effective-learners-must-become-our-aim/

Martin, A.J. (2016) *Using Load Reduction Instruction (LRI) to Boost Motivation and Engagement*. Leicester: British Psychological Society.

Monbiot, G. (2017, 15 February) In an age of robots, schools are teaching our children to be redundant. Retrieved from: www.theguardian.com/commentisfree/2017/feb/15/robots-schools-teaching-children-redundant-testing-learn-future

Mylrea, H. (2017, 17 August) Jeremy Clarkson is back with his annual reminder that grades aren't everything. Retrieved from: www.nme.com/blogs/nme-blogs/jeremy-clarkson-annual-reminder-grades-arent-everything-2125647

Nation, K. (2019) Children's reading difficulties, language, and reflections on the simple view of reading. *Australian Journal of Learning Difficulties*, 24(1): 47–73.

Newmark, B. (2020, 28 April) Pile on! (Blog post). Retrieved from: https://bennewmark.wordpress.com/2020/04/28/pile-on/

Ohlsson, S. (2009) Resubsumption: A possible mechanism for conceptual change and belief revision. *Educational Psychologist*, 44(1): 20–40.

Pekrun, R., Lichtenfeld, S., Marsh, H.W., Murayama, K. and Goetz, T. (2017) Achievement, emotions and academic performance: Longitudinal models of reciprocal effects. *Child Development*, 88(5): 1653–70. Retrieved from: https://doi.org/10.1111/cdev. 12704

Perkins, D. (2014) *Future Wise: Educating our Children for a Changing World*. Chichester: John Wiley & Sons.

Perry, M. (2020) Pluriversal literacies: Affect and relationality in vulnerable times. *Reading Research Quarterly*. Retrieved from: https://doi.org/10.1002/rrq.312

Plutarch (1927) *De auditu* (On listening to lectures). In *Moralia*, trans. F.C. Babbitt (Loeb Classical Library). Available online at: penelope.uchicago.edu/Thayer/E/Roman/Texts/Plutarch/Moralia/ (accessed 13 September 2013).

Ramsburg, J.T. and Ohlsson, S. (2016) Category change in the absence of cognitive conflict. *Journal of Educational Psychology*, 108(1): 98.

Ronson, J. (2015, 12 February) How one stupid tweet blew up Justine Sacco's life. *The New York Times Magazine*. Retrieved from: www.nytimes.com/2015/02/15/magazine/how-one-stupid-tweet-ruined-justine-saccos-life.html

Shemilt, S. (2015, 26 March) Cricket World Cup 2015: Australia beat India to reach final. Retrieved from: www.bbc.com/sport/cricket/32065108

Waterhouse, L. (2006) Inadequate evidence for multiple intelligences, Mozart effect, and emotional intelligence theories. *Educational Psychologist*, 41(4): 247–55.

Yu, S. and Levesque-Bristol, C. (2020) A cross-classified path analysis of the self-determination theory model on the situational, individual and classroom levels in college education. *Contemporary Educational Psychology*, 101857.

2

DIRECT AND EXPLICIT

Key Points

- Direct Instruction is a specific kind of explicit teaching that uses scripted lessons.
- Explicit teaching is a whole system and not just an episode within a lesson, although we should be cautious about reducing it to a checklist.
- There is strong evidence for explicit teaching from a range of sources such as process-product research and the experiments of cognitive load theory.
- Explicit teaching is unpopular with many in education because it conflicts with popular theories.

Introduction

In 1967, President Lyndon Johnson rose to deliver the annual State of the Union address to the United States Congress and to announce a new front in the war on poverty (Evans, 1981). The Head Start programme for disadvantaged pre-school children was going to be expanded into the early grades of school. Johnson was planning a budget of over $100 million, but Congress ultimately slashed this to just $15 million. This provoked a rethink and the project was redesigned as a research programme. 'Follow Through' was born. Despite the circumstances of its inception, it grew to become the largest and most expensive education research project ever undertaken.

The study had a classic 'horse-race' design. Different sponsors were engaged to deliver programmes and the results of these programmes were to be evaluated against each other and against the results gained by similar students who were not part of the project – i.e. the 'control'. Many of the sponsors used so-called 'child-centred' approaches (Bereiter and Kurland, 1981). This is a misnomer because all teaching is, by definition, child-centred. Nevertheless, these sponsors' programmes were distinguished by giving students choices about their learning, often based on the constructivist teaching philosophy that children were assumed to need to construct their own meaning.

A few sponsors took a very different approach. Some emphasised certain basic skills such as sounding-out words or arithmetic. Children were required to master these before moving on to higher level tasks. One such programme was the clear winner of the horse-race: Direct Instruction.

Developed by Siegfried Engelmann and Wesley Becker, Direct Instruction is far from a traditional or standard approach to teaching. The environment is highly controlled, with the sequencing of concepts decided by the programme's developers to the point where lessons themselves are scripted for the teachers. The scripting of lessons is perhaps the best-known feature of Direct Instruction. However, when interviewed about this aspect, Engelmann suggested that it evolved out of the practical issues of ensuring the intervention was delivered faithfully rather than being identified as necessary and desirable from the outset (Boulton, 2009).

Scripted lessons arose because Engelmann diverges from mainstream thinking. To Engelmann, 'there's a great difference between teaching and designing effective instruction' (Barbash, 2012). Planning lessons and delivering lessons require different skills. Traditionally, the same person does both because these skills are seen as complementary, but in Direct Instruction programmes, planning and delivery are conceived as separate tasks. Lesson planners decide on the responses that they want the children to give and teachers reinforce these with praise.

From basic skills to a life of crime

The fact that Direct Instruction was labelled as a 'basic skills' programme has perhaps led to a misconception – that Direct Instruction was shown to be good for – and *only* good for – developing basic skills. In fact, Follow Through assessed a range of different measures. Not only did Direct Instruction produce the greatest gains compared to control groups in basic skills, it also produced large gains in problem-solving skills and self-esteem. Many of the other programmes performed worse than the control. Most of the child-centred approaches actually underperformed the control for basic skills and problem-solving skills. Quite a few programmes that emphasised self-esteem performed worse than the control on measures of self-esteem.

Follow Through has been the subject of sustained criticism. Much of this has been aimed at the methodology of the study which was big and messy. The fact that it was both an intervention and an experiment led to difficulties in controlling variables. Larger differences were found between different schools using the same model than between different models in the same school.

Other critics draw unfavourable characterisations of Direct Instruction, query the measures used or even question the strategy of trying to apply a scientific approach to education research (House et al., 1978). Education commentator Alfie Kohn has reiterated similar points and has questioned whether any initial gains from Direct Instruction would be sustained over time (Kohn, 2000). Nevertheless, a study by Linda Meyer (1984) located Direct Instruction and control group students many years after the intervention, and found a positive correlation between Direct Instruction and desirable outcomes such as graduation rates and later achievement.

One particular body of research by Lawrence Schweinhart, David Wiekart and others (1986) – which is often cited (e.g. Gray, 2015) – purports to show that Direct Instruction (also known as 'Distar') in preschool led to increased involvement in crime in adolescence:

> According to self-reports at age 15, the group that had attended the Distar preschool program engaged in twice as many delinquent acts as did the other two curriculum groups, including five times as many acts of property violence. The Distar group also reported relatively poor relations with their families, less participation in sports, fewer school job appointments, and less reaching out to others for help with personal problems. These findings, based on one study with a small sample, are by no means definitive; but they do suggest possible consequences of preschool curriculum models that ought to be considered.

This finding is extraordinary. If true, it would not only represent a particularly long-lasting cause-and-effect relationship, but also a 'transfer' effect: we might perhaps expect an academic training programme to have a long-term effect on academic performance, but it is far more surprising that it has crossed domains and had an effect on criminal behaviour.

Self-reports are not always the strongest form of evidence in educational research and Carl Bereiter (1986), an ex-colleague of Engelmann, suggests that a lack of detail about the procedures used in the Schweinhart et al. research calls it further into question. Bereiter also suggests that the differences that were found were not statistically significant and were biased due to the gender representation in the different groups – there were a greater proportion of males in the Direct Instruction group and that they tend to commit a greater number of the kinds of crimes captured by the self-report questions.

Direct Instruction researcher Martin Kozloff (2011) makes the following comments:

> Let us ignore the fact that instead of reporting the actual rates of antisocial behavior, Schweinhart and Weikart generally report percentages; e.g., that there was allegedly twice as much antisocial behavior among prior DI kids twenty years later. Let us also ignore the fact that these percentage differences actually

amount to differences in the activities of only one or two persons. What is most telling, and just plain bizarre, is that these two writers barely entertain the possibility that: (1) a dozen years of school experience; (2) area of residence; (3) family background; (4) the influence of gangs; and (5) differential economic opportunity, had anything to do with adolescent development and adult behavior.

Perhaps the best answer to all of the Follow Through critics is again supplied by Bereiter and Kurland (1981). They draw our attention to the lack of effect of many of the 'child-centered' models:

> When child-centered educators purport to increase the self-esteem of disadvantaged children and yet fail to show evidence of this on the Coopersmith Self-Concept Inventory, we may ask what real and substantial changes in self-esteem would one expect to occur that would not be reflected in changes on the Coopersmith? Similarly, for reasoning and problem-solving. If no evidence of effect shows on a test of non-verbal reasoning, or a reading comprehension test loaded with inferential questions, or on a mathematical problem-solving test, we must ask why not? What kinds of real, fundamental improvements in logical reasoning abilities would fail to be reflected in any of these tests?

Explicit teaching

These days, the term 'direct instruction' is used interchangeably to mean Engelmann and Becker's approach, any highly structured, teacher-directed programme based upon explanation, demonstration and practice, and also as a pejorative term to describe situations where a teacher lectures and students sit and listen 'passively' (Rosenshine, 2008). But Engelmann and Becker's approach is distinctive, not least due to the scripting of lessons and ordering of concepts. Not all forms of explicit teaching would share these features. To try to avoid confusion, I will use 'Direct Instruction' or 'Big DI' to refer to Engelmann and Becker's specific approach and 'explicit instruction' or 'explicit teaching' to refer to structured direct instruction more generally.

The principles of Direct Instruction are set out in a epic tome written by Siegfried Engelmann and Douglas Carnine in 1982, *Theory of Instruction: Principles and Applications*. A full discussion of Big DI is beyond the scope of this book. It is a highly structured approach that follows a set methodology according to a number of key principles. Some of these are not intuitive but make intuitive sense once you learn about them. For instance, Big DI makes extensive use of non-examples. A non-example is an example of what something is *not*. A teacher could perhaps present the letter 'P' and say, 'This is a P', then a lower case 'p' and say, 'This is a P', then perhaps 'P' but in red ink and say, 'This is a P' before presenting 'F' and saying, 'This is *not* a P'. Many errors that students make stem from overgeneralisations (Ryan and Williams, 2007), such as overgeneralising from the fact that $\frac{1}{4}$ is smaller than $\frac{1}{3}$ to conclude that the larger the denominator in a fraction, the smaller the fraction and therefore thinking $\frac{11}{12}$ is smaller than $\frac{2}{3}$. So, a formal process of clearly defining the boundaries of concepts makes a lot of sense. Non-examples are part of a wider aim to faultlessly communicate concepts from the outset in such a way that misconceptions will not develop. However, Big DI doesn't just sprinkle in ideas such as non-examples, they are built into a consistent theory around precisely how to order examples, depending on the nature of the concepts to be learnt.

The principles in *Theory of Instruction* are derived from many years of painstaking action research as Engelmann and his various collaborators sought to refine Big DI programmes. Although these principles make intuitive sense, and although I personally find the case for them to be highly persuasive, it is hard to say exactly how effective they make Big DI, especially when compared to other explicit teaching programmes. A recent meta-analysis of Big DI curricula (Stockard et al., 2018) found consistently positive effects on achievement. However, the fact that Big DI is unpopular with mainstream education academics means that these studies were mainly conducted by a relatively small pool of researchers associated with Big DI. As always with meta-analysis, a range of different control conditions were used – Big DI was compared to lots of different alternatives – and so such a meta-analysis provides little direct evidence that the specific practices that differentiate Big DI from explicit instruction more generally generate a positive effect.

You might perhaps expect educationalists to highlight the problems in the methodology of Project Follow Through. This is an obvious point of weakness and the findings are perhaps unpalatable to those who are ideologically inclined towards so-called 'child-centered' approaches. What I find surprising, however, is the number of people involved in education and education research who seem to have *never even heard of* Follow Through. Moreover, they also seem largely unaware of the larger field of study it is often associated with: process–product education research that ran from roughly the 1950s until the early 1980s. This body of work largely corroborates the findings of Follow Through while adding evidence for structured explicit teaching more generally.

Process–product studies involved researchers observing classrooms and various teacher behaviours. They then sought to correlate the behaviours they observed with student learning gains. In other words, they sought to address the question of which teacher behaviours were associated with more student progress. The results of such process–product studies are therefore a series of correlations, so we should be careful before we suggest that we have identified a cause. For instance, imagine that we find that teachers who write learning objectives on the whiteboard at the start of a lesson tend to have greater student progress. We may assume that writing learning objectives on the board *causes* the greater progress. However, it is possible that some other factor causes both. Perhaps teachers who are better organised tend to write learning objectives on the board and their superior organisation is what leads to the learning gains. However, the process–product research is extensive and, as we will see, its key findings are supported by other forms of research.

In 1984, Jere Brophy and Thomas Good summarised a large corpus of process–product research as a chapter for Wittrock's *Handbook of Research on Teaching* (Brophy and Good, 1986). In 2015, Good delivered a conference paper on the topic titled 'Research on teaching: Yesterday, today, and tomorrow' (Good, 2015). In this paper, he outlines some of the key findings from process–product studies. He lists the teacher behaviours that are frequently associated with student learning gains. The list includes effective use of time; a coherent curriculum in sequence; active teaching – 'Do teachers actively present concepts and supervise students' initial work, and then encourage them to build and to extend meaningfully on teachers' initial presentations?' – a balance between conceptual and procedural knowledge; proactive management; teacher clarity, enthusiasm and warmth; pace; teaching to mastery; review and feedback; and teachers' possession of adequate subject matter knowledge.

These are the key features of effective explicit instruction. Notice that the role of the teacher is vital. In these classrooms, students don't select their own learning activities. The teacher's role is not to facilitate and guide, but to fully direct the learning. Explicit teaching is planned and sequenced. In contrast with the common caricature of explicit teaching as a dreary drill, Good emphasises that the most successful teachers are able to teach with warmth and enjoy good relationships with their students.

Good warns against using his list of characteristics as some kind of checklist or rubric against which to measure teachers – we shall see why this is good advice later. Good also reflects on some of his regrets as he neared the end of his career, warning us against faddism:

> Much like research on teaching (but to a greater extent) educational reform/innovation moves from one simple conception of the problem to another simple conception of the problem (and its solution) without much evidence. Further there is wide consensus that the major educational reforms have been extremely costly but notably unproductive . . . in addition to the large reform movements encouraged by government and policy papers there have been field-initiated reforms that recommend the desirability of particular methods and that were seen as a panacea by some and sometimes for a sustained period of time.

Good also notes that strong findings from education research – such as those from the process–product studies – are often forgotten or ignored by the field:

> Alyson Lavigne and I commented on several recent studies suggesting that they had provided new contributions linking teacher actions to student achievements. In particular, we mentioned studies that had highlighted findings very close to process-product findings reviewed by Brophy & Good (1986) and, at least implicitly, suggesting that these were new findings.

There we also noted that Hattie (2009) had not mentioned process-product studies including its experimental contributions. ⌈Some references removed.⌉

Good is particularly concerned about teacher education and the fact that it does not seem to adequately prepare teachers for the classroom:

> it would seem important for teacher education programs to assure that their graduates, in addition to possessing appropriate content information and a thorough understanding of how students learn and develop, would also have clear conceptual understanding and skills related to active teaching, proactive management, communication of appropriate expectations for learning and the ability to plan and deliver instruction that balances procedural and conceptual knowledge. I have no way of knowing whether this information is actively taught in the curriculum and if it is taught, the extent to which it is presented as a perspective needing interpretation and sensitivity to context . . . . Yet, the continuing evidence reporting that many beginning teachers have considerable difficulty in managing classrooms suggests that the research on teaching that I describe here has not been well integrated into teacher education programs.

Barak Rosenshine (2009), who was involved in process–product research in the 1970s, argues that it is not just process–product research that supports the use of explicit forms of teaching. Rosenshine notes that research from the 1970s and 1980s into the teaching of 'ill-structured' tasks also validates explicit approaches:

> These procedures come from the large body of experimental studies, all involving teacher-led instruction, that have been successful in teaching reading comprehension, mathematical problem solving, writing, science problem solving, and study skills as measured by standardized tests and experimenter-developed tests.

It is an interesting and separate question as to the amount of time teachers should spend attempting to directly teach reading comprehension strategies or skills (see e.g. Willingham, 2006), but if this is the aim, then we have evidence to support using an explicit approach.

Rosenshine is now perhaps best known for his 'Principles of instruction' (2012), a brief paper that has recently been the subject of a book by Tom Sherrington (2019). Rosenshine avoids the term 'direct instruction' throughout, perhaps mindful of its many different interpretations, but his principles provide a good working definition of the form of explicit teaching that is supported by the process–product research literature. It is also clear that Rosenshine is talking about a whole system of gradual transfer from teacher to student. For example, effective teachers frequently revisit previous learning, present new material in short steps with lots of student practice, constantly check for understanding, and guide students through shared practice and into independent practice. To paraphrase crudely, Rosenshine's principles progress from 'I do' to 'we do' to 'you do'.

Many of the pedagogical fashions of recent years, such as project-based learning or enquiry learning, are clearly at odds with these principles. Nevertheless, adherents often claim to use explicit teaching as part of such an approach. Whatever they mean by this, be it short periods of lecturing or explicit teaching after a principle has been figured out by the students, they cannot mean the kind of explicit teaching that is supported by the evidence that Rosenshine draws upon. A form of explicit teaching that is aligned with this evidence cannot be an event or a section of a lesson, but a whole system that incorporates planning and teaching over the short, medium and long term. If project-based learning or enquiry learning are supported by evidence, it is not this evidence.

Clipboards and checklists

In recent years, it has become clear through social media that some teachers who have heard of Rosenshine's principles have experimented with building them in to lesson observation tools. At this point, we need to return to Thomas Good's warning. There is nothing intrinsically wrong with examining what a teacher does in the classroom, but we must be cautious before we start making judgements on the basis of these observations. The teachers who were the subjects of process–product research did not know what the results of this research would find, but we do. There is an adage known as 'Goodhart's Law', named after the economist John Goodhart and originating in monetary policy, that is often stated as 'when a measure becomes a target, it ceases to be a good measure' (Strathern, 1997). This problem seems to have bedevilled attempts to evaluate teacher performance through the use of lesson observation (Coe, 2014).

Why might this be? One possible reason is that teaching is a complex process involving the interaction of many behaviours. Some of these behaviours – such as asking a lot of questions and checking the responses of all students – may be a good proxy indicator for a wider set of behaviours and understandings. However, once teachers know that the *goal* is to ask lots of questions and that they will be evaluated on whether or not they do this, then they may engage in this activity without the wider behaviours and understandings.

This is a common problem in all evaluation rubrics that are developed for assessing performance in a complex domain (Figure 2.1):

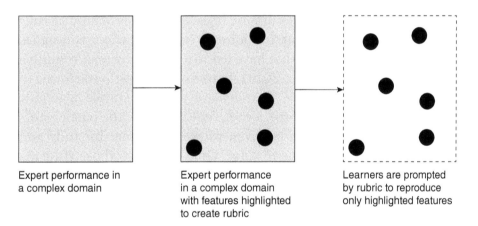

Expert performance in a complex domain

Expert performance in a complex domain with features highlighted to create rubric

Learners are prompted by rubric to reproduce only highlighted features

Figure 2.1 How rubrics fail

There are a number of possible ways to deal with a problem of this kind. First, we could develop a rubric to evaluate teaching, but then not tell teachers what is on that rubric. Such an approach seems both disrespectful and unfeasible – teachers would clearly find out after a few rounds of feedback. Alternatively, we could go down Engelmann's route and script each detail of a lesson, including when to ask questions and how – all any observer would then need to monitor is the level of adherence to the script alongside factors such as pace, prosody, enthusiasm, and so on. Finally, we could seek to build a broader understanding of what we want teachers to achieve by developing a wider knowledge of the relevant research, including some of the more basic educational psychology evidence that underpins explicit teaching. Teaching would be less about reproducing certain selected features of effective instruction but about applying a set of underlying concepts about learning. Although of less appeal to a clipboard-wielding bureaucrat due to the essentially unobservable nature of these underlying concepts, this final option may be capable of producing enduring change in classrooms where scripted lessons are not an option.

Lab or classroom?

So, what are the underlying concepts that teachers should understand? The third body of evidence that Rosenshine cites – evidence from shorter, experimental studies – support many of the individual principles he lists and can lead teachers to a broader understanding of how learning occurs. Key among these are a series of studies conducted by Australian researcher John Sweller and various colleagues from the 1980s onwards that have led to a field known as 'cognitive load theory' (Sweller et al., 2019). In one of the most basic forms of these experiments, novice learners are given a simple algebraic equation to solve of the form, $ax = b$, find x. Half of the participants are randomly assigned to be given worked examples to study and half are assigned problems to solve. On a later test, those students given worked examples to study – which provide explicit instruction in how to solve the problem – perform better than those who are given problems to solve. This result has now been replicated in diverse fields of learning. For instance, a 'worked example' in the form of an annotated version of a Shakespeare play (Oksa et al., 2010) has been shown to have a similar, positive effect on learning. Similarly, undergraduate chemistry students studying a completed concept map learnt more than those who had to complete part of the concept map themselves (Wong et al., 2020).

These worked-example studies may seem artificial in their design – something that is often necessary in order to have a well-controlled experiment. There is a trade-off here: we can have messy, authentic classroom situations such as in Project Follow Through and complain about the messiness, or we can have rigorously controlled experiments such as those conducted by Sweller and complain about their inauthenticity. The findings, however, seem to point in the same direction.

And when discussing cognitive load theory, we must not fall into a trap of assuming that it has only been tested in clinical settings at universities. For instance, Alison Peacock, head of England's Chartered College of Teaching, claimed in an interview in 2019 that cognitive load theory is 'not research based on school-age children' (Roberts, 2019). After John Sweller pointed out that, in fact, a large amount of cognitive load theory research had been conducted with school-age children, Peacock retracted her claim (George, 2019).

An experiment that perhaps represents a good balance between the two extremes of clinical research versus messy, real-world research was carried out in the Netherlands and examined the most effective ways to intervene with students who are struggling in mathematics (Kroesbergen et al., 2004). The elementary school students, including some who attended special schools, were randomly assigned to one of three groups: the first group were given a series of 'constructivist' intervention lessons where different students' problem-solving approaches were surfaced and discussed. The second group were given the same number of intervention lessons based on an explicit model where standard methods were fully explained by the teacher. The third group were given no intervention at all. Both intervention groups made more progress than those students who had no intervention, but the explicit instruction group made more progress than the constructivist group.

It is important to note that the students benefited from *both* interventions. Perhaps simply practising more maths has an effect or perhaps the knowledge that you are in an intervention leads to a placebo-like effect. So, we should always be cautious when a single intervention is compared with no intervention at all – it doesn't prove much. Unfortunately, the education research literature is replete with studies that compare doing something with doing nothing, and these studies are often the basis of claims that 'research shows' a particular approach works. Imagine the study described above but without the explicit teaching condition and with just the constructivist condition compared to no intervention. It is not hard to picture this result being used to claim that research shows the constructivist approach works. When evaluating research, it is always important to consider what the intervention is being compared against. Is it the best possible alternative?

Struggling to understand

Whatever evidence may accrue for explicit teaching, there remains the possibility that even if alternatives to explicit teaching lead to less short-term learning, the struggle involved on the part of the students means that they will learn the principles *better*, that this will lead to a deeper form of learning. This is hard to test. What is the definition of 'deeper' learning? For instance, do we not consider the better problem-solving performance of the Direct Instruction students in Follow Through as evidence of deeper learning?

David Klahr and Milena Nigam have completed a series of studies aimed at addressing the question of whether different teaching methods suit different objectives. In one such study, students were randomly assigned to one of two groups (Klahr and Nigam, 2004). The first group were given explicit teaching in a key scientific principle – the need to control variables. The second group were given suitable equipment to explore the issue and discover the principle for themselves. Unsurprisingly, given the evidence so far presented, more students in the first group learnt the principle. However, the students were later asked to judge science fair posters produced by others – a significant part of such an evaluation is whether the posters demonstrate a fair test with controlled variables. The key finding was that students who had managed to discover the principle for themselves were no better at evaluating the posters than students who had learnt the principle through explicit instruction.

If there are those who wish to claim that there are objectives for which alternatives to explicit teaching are superior, then the burden of proof perhaps lies with them. As Bertrand Russell famously argued, it is entirely possible that a teapot, too small to be seen by telescopes, orbits the Sun somewhere in space between the Earth and Mars. However, it is the burden of anyone making this claim to prove its existence. It is not the burden of the sceptic to prove its non-existence (Russell, 1952).

Unknown and forgotten

Thomas Good is right to be concerned that a significant amount of research evidence is not reflected in the way we train teachers. We can perhaps shed a little light on why if we consider studies discussed by Gregory Yates from the University of South Australia (Yates, 2005). Yates summarises findings from process–product and teacher expertise research, all of which is in line with the teacher behaviours identified by Good. Indeed, Yates suggests that teacher expertise research shows that expert teaching is characterised by 'Remarkably complete explanations executed quickly then students move into active practice under strong guidance' and that process–product research shows that highly effective classrooms involve a 'user-friendly direct instruction teaching cycle to teach both content and process' (i.e. what and how to think).

Yates links this to David Berliner's 'simple theory' of classroom instruction based on engagement time and academic learning time. However, the most telling part of the paper is a small investigation conducted by Yates himself by surveying student teachers:

> The following question is embedded within one such paper: What are the traits of highly effective teachers? In 2004 I sampled responses on this item from 100 students, all university graduates from a range of disciplines, undergoing training to become teachers . . . . Not one of the 100 papers sampled was allocated full marks on that item. Not a single student cited the effective teacher's ability to articulate clearly, or to get students to maintain time engagement. The majority of responses described the more humanistic side of teaching, articulating the belief that effective teachers are warm, friendly, positive human beings. But such traits can be considered basic for all teachers, rather than traits associated specifically with achievement effectiveness criteria.

It is astonishing to contemplate that teachers who are being educated today may not be aware of such a relevant finding from a large corpus of research. Why might this be? Either our teacher education institutions are institutionally forgetful or there is something about the findings that makes teacher educators reluctant to share them. In truth, it is probably a little of both.

Education certainly does seem to be subjected to fashions and fads in the way that Good describes. This churn – this constant recycling – makes it hard for the field to hold on to its memories. If it did, then we might expect progress rather than the repetition of previous mistakes.

But there are also deep, philosophical reasons why so many in education dislike explicit teaching. It is viewed as authoritarian and antidemocratic. Instead of having knowledge imposed upon them, students would be better to come to know things for themselves. The role of the teacher is therefore to suitably arrange the artefacts of instruction in order to encourage and guide this 'growth'. It is an idea expressed by the influential philosopher of education, John Dewey, in his 1916 work *Democracy and Education*:

> The development within the young of the attitudes and dispositions necessary to the continuous and progressive life of a society cannot take place by direct conveyance of beliefs, emotions, and knowledge. It takes place through the intermediary of the environment. The environment consists of the sum total of conditions which are concerned in the execution of the activity characteristic of a living being. The social environment consists of all the activities of fellow beings that are bound up in the carrying on of the activities of any one of its members. It is truly educative in its effect in the degree in which an individual shares or participates in some conjoint activity. By doing his share in the associated activity, the individual appropriates the purpose which actuates it, becomes familiar with its methods and subject matters, acquires needed skill, and is saturated with its emotional spirit.

Dewey is neither the first nor the last to have expressed such sentiments but Dewey is especially influential. He has achieved a status such that any attempt at interpreting his work is often met with stern criticism, an issue compounded by the fact that Dewey's ideas seem to have evolved over time. Scholars argue over different interpretations of his work much as theologians may argue over opaque passages from the Bible. For instance, in 1980, Kieran Egan of Simon Fraser University wrote an academic paper arguing that Dewey had negatively influenced the social studies curriculum in the US by encouraging an 'expanding horizons' model (Egan, 1980). This is a model that starts with the child and works outwards: the first steps in history education are to explore the child's family relationships; the first steps in geography are to examine the local area, and so on.

Egan's case was that this had led to an excessively dull curriculum. Moreover, the idea that children cannot cope with concepts that are far away in culture and time is flawed:

If one considers what most engages children's minds it is surely stories about monsters, witches, dragons, knights and princesses in distant times and places, rather than the subject-matter, however actively engaged, of families, local environments, and communities. Children clearly do not have to be led from their everyday reality by a process of expanding horizons till they gain access to talking animals in bizarre places and strange times. It is clear that children have direct access to their curious imaginary realms. Indeed, they have much easier access to these than to the content of their everyday world when it is treated as 'subject-matter.'

Egan pre-empted the criticism that he had misunderstood Dewey and yet he was, in due course, subjected to exactly such a criticism (Thornton, 1984). Don't disrespect Dewey.

Dewey's continuing influence is perhaps best demonstrated by the fact that, penned in 1980, Egan's critique was drawing on criticism of the social studies curriculum that stretched as far back as the 1960s, yet the recently revised Australian curriculum (Australian Curriculum, Assessment and Reporting Authority, 2015) uses exactly Dewey's expanding horizons model.

It cannot just be ignorance or philosophical conviction that keeps explicit instruction off the agenda. There has to be more to it and it has to operate in everyday classrooms and not just colleges of teacher education.

A conspiracy theory

My own feeling is that much of what goes on in the classrooms of secondary schools is a suboptimal kind of explicit instruction. I have observed many lessons in two different countries – England and Australia – as well as having taught my own. Teachers do tend to use group work and a variety of activities, but there is still a lot of standing at the front and instructing the class. I would suggest that it is suboptimal because it's rarely explicit *enough*. However, this is a difficult issue to address in a culture that is hostile to being explicit *at all*.

If you read a teachers' guide for one of Siegfried Engelmann's programmes, you will see that everything is planned and structured meticulously and everything is explained to the students. As a teacher reading it, my sense is almost as if *too much* is explained. Teaching in the wild – the kind of teaching that actually goes on in ordinary classrooms – relies more on inference and hints. Teachers play the 'guess what's in my head' game under the misconception that it is better for students to come to a realisation for themselves. Explanations are rarely rehearsed, although they do evolve as a teacher reteaches the course.

I have a routine at the start of my lessons. I draw a box on the whiteboard and students pick up the board pen and write down any homework questions they struggled with. I have been doing this for a long time and yet I am *always* surprised and, if I am honest, often quietly annoyed. Issues arise that I thought I had pre-empted with a good explanation. How can they possibly not understand *this*?

The Dunning–Kruger effect (Kruger and Dunning, 1999) is a cognitive bias where a relatively unskilled individual overestimates their level of skill within a particular area. It is thought to arise because the individual lacks the knowledge needed for accurate calibration. If we don't know what expert performance looks like then we won't realise that we are lacking that expertise. We don't know what we don't know.

The inverse of the Dunning–Kruger effect is the curse of knowledge (Birch and Bloom, 2007), a related cognitive bias, and is effectively a failure of empathy. If you know something, then it is hard to imagine yourself into a mind that does not know it. The curse of knowledge is probably related to the ease with which we draw on, and process, knowledge held in long-term memory (Sweller et al., 2019). The effortlessness of retrieval from long-term memory leads us to assume that we are not actually doing anything and that everyone else is capable of the same.

What happens when teachers suffering from the curse of knowledge teach students suffering from the Dunning–Kruger effect? The danger is an unwitting conspiracy: the teacher thinks their students understand and the students think they understand, but the students *don't* understand and, perhaps more pertinently, they are unable to demonstrate understanding by answering relevant questions or completing relevant tasks.

Perhaps this is why explicit teaching is so effective. When we choose to follow a process that makes us examine the individual elements we are attempting to teach and then constantly check whether students have grasped them, there is no void remaining to be filled by these biases. If I am forced to think through, step-by-step, the process I want students to follow, then I am confronted by the assumptions I am taking into the classroom. If I ask for feedback on the homework or regularly check the understanding of all of my students, I cannot fool myself into thinking they must have learnt something when they have not.

And perhaps this is explicit teaching's undoing. A nuts-and-bolts approach seems too agricultural, lacking in sophistication. Education, an academic domain with an inferiority complex, wants to be seen as on a par with other fields – that is why the pseudo-profound and pseudo-mystical has its appeal. Surgeons and engineers know their worth and so can specify, at great length, precisely how to perform a hip replacement or construct a particular type of truss without fear of being labelled as mere technicians. But education is striving for something more. It wants to talk of French philosophers and grand struggles against oppression, which is not the most effective way to teach children how to balance chemical equations one excruciating step at a time.

References

Australian Curriculum, Assessment and Reporting Authority (2015) *Annual Report: Foundation to Year 10 Curriculum: Humanities and the Social Sciences*. Sydney, Australia.

Barbash, S. (2012) Clear teaching. Arlington, VT: Education Consumers Foundation.

Bereiter, C. (1986) Does direct instruction cause delinquency? *Early Childhood Research Quarterly*, 1(3): 289–92.

Bereiter, C. and Kurland, M. (1981) A constructive look at Follow Through results. *Interchange on Educational Policy*, 12(1): 1–22.

Birch, S.A. and Bloom, P. (2007) The curse of knowledge in reasoning about false beliefs. *Psychological Science*, 18(5): 382–6.

Boulton, D. (2009) Siegfried Engelmann: Instructional Design 101: Learn from the learners! *Children of the Code*. Retrieved from: https://childrenofthecode.org/interviews/engelmann.htm

Brophy, J. and Good T. (1986) Teacher behavior and student achievement. In Wittrock, M. (ed.), *Handbook on Research in Teaching* (3rd edn). New York: Macmillan, pp. 328–75.

Coe, R. (2014) Classroom observation: it's harder than you think. *CEM Blog*. Retrieved from: www.cem.org/blog/414/

Dewey, J. (1916) *Democracy and Education: An Introduction to the Philosophy of Education*. New York: Macmillan.

Egan, K. (1980). John Dewey and the social studies curriculum. *Theory & Research in Social Education*, 8(2): 37–55.

Engelmann, S. and Carnine, D. (1982) *Theory of Instruction: Principles and Applications*. New York: Irvington.

Evans, J.W. (1981) What have we learned from Follow Through? Implications for future R & D programs. ERIC: Institute of Education Science. Available at: eric.ed.gov

George, M. (2019, January) Chartered College backtracks on Ofsted research criticism. *Tes*. Retrieved from: www.tes.com/news/chartered-college-backtracks-ofsted-research-criticism

Good, T.L. (2015, January) *Research on Teaching: Yesterday, Today, and Tomorrow*. Paper presented at the International Congress for School Effectiveness and Improvement, Cincinnati, Ohio.

Gray, P. (2015) Early academic training produces long-term harm. *Psychology Today*. Retrieved from: www.psychologytoday.com/au/blog/freedom-learn/201505/early-academic-training-produces-long-term-harm

Hattie, J.A.C. (2009) *Visible Learning: A Synthesis of 800+ Meta-analyses on Achievement*. Abingdon: Routledge.

House, E., Glass, G., McLean, L. and Walker, D. (1978) No simple answer: Critique of the Follow Through evaluation. *Harvard Educational Review*, 48(2): 128–60.

Klahr, D. and Nigam, M. (2004) The equivalence of learning paths in early science instruction effects of direct instruction and discovery learning. *Psychological Science*, 15(10): 661–7.

Kohn, A. (2000) *The Schools our Children Deserve: Moving Beyond Traditional Classrooms and "Tougher Standards"*. Boston, MA: Houghton Mifflin Harcourt.

Kozloff, M. (2011) DI creates felons, but literate ones. Contribution to the DI Listserve, University of Oregon, 31 December.

Kroesbergen, E.H., Van Luit, J.E. and Maas, C.J. (2004) Effectiveness of explicit and constructivist mathematics instruction for low-achieving students in the Netherlands. *The Elementary School Journal*, 233–51.

Kruger, J. and Dunning, D. (1999) Unskilled and unaware of it: How difficulties in recognizing one's own incompetence lead to inflated self-assessments. *Journal of Personality and Social Psychology*, 77(6): 1121.

Meyer, L.A. (1984) Long-term academic effects of the direct instruction Project Follow Through. *The Elementary School Journal*, 380–94.

Oksa, A., Kalyuga, S. and Chandler, P. (2010) Expertise reversal effect in using explanatory notes for readers of Shakespearean text. *Instructional Science*, 38(3): 217–36.

Roberts, J. (2019, January) Exclusive: Ofsted research for new inspections 'based on uni students'. *Tes*. Retrieved from: www.tes.com/news/exclusive-ofsted-research-new-inspections-based-uni-students

Rosenshine, B. (2008) Five meanings of direct instruction. Lincoln: Center on Innovation & Improvement.

Rosenshine, B. (2009) The empirical support for direct instruction. In Tobias, S. and Duffy, T.M. (eds) *Constructivist Instruction: Success or Failure?* New York: Routledge.

Rosenshine, B. (2012) Principles of instruction: Research-based strategies that all teachers should know. *American Educator*, 36(1): 12.

Russell, B. (1952) Is there a God? Commissioned but not published by *Illustrated* magazine.

Ryan, J. and Williams, J. (2007) *Children's Mathematics 4–15: Learning from Errors and Misconceptions*. New York: McGraw-Hill.

Schweinhart, L.L., Weikart, D.P. and Larner, M.B. Consequences of three preschool curriculum models through age 15. *Early Childhood Research Quarterly*, 1(1): 15–45.

Sherrington, T. (2019) *Rosenshine's Principles in Action*. Woodbridge: John Catt Educational.

Stockard, J., Wood, T.W., Coughlin, C. and Rasplica Khoury, C. (2018) The effectiveness of direct instruction curricula: A meta-analysis of a half century of research. *Review of Educational Research*, 88(4): 479–507.

Strathern, M. (1997) 'Improving ratings': audit in the British University system. *European Review*, 5(3): 305–21.

Sweller, J., van Merriënboer, J.J. and Paas, F. (2019) Cognitive architecture and instructional design: 20 years later. *Educational Psychology Review*, 1–32.

Thornton, S.J. (1984) Social studies misunderstood: A reply to Kieran Egan. *Theory & Research in Social Education*, 12(1): 43–7.

Willingham, D.T. (2006) The usefulness of brief instruction in reading comprehension strategies. *American Educator*, 30(4): 39–50.

Wong, R.M., Sundararajan, N., Adesope, O.O. and Nishida, K.R. (2020) Static and interactive concept maps for chemistry learning. *Educational Psychology*. doi.org.10.1080/01443410.2020.1761299

Yates, G.C. (2005) "How Obvious": Personal reflections on the database of educational psychology and effective teaching research. *Educational Psychology*, 25(6): 681–700.

3

BOTTOM-UP OR TOP-DOWN?

Key Points

- A top-down process of education involves emulating the behaviours of experts in the hope of becoming more expert.
- A bottom-up process of education involves breaking expert performance down into small components and teaching these first before reintegrating them.
- Bottom-up processes are superior for complex academic learning.
- We can understand the effectiveness of bottom-up processes through the model of the mind used by cognitive load theory.

Introduction

Imagine you join a gym. You arrive for your orientation with one of the coaches at the gym who is going to teach you how to use the equipment. First, is the leg press. The coach adjusts the length and number of weights, sits on the leg press and demonstrates how she wants you to use it, where your back should rest and so on, explaining the rationale for these instructions as she goes. She gets up and gestures to the equipment with her hand. You follow her approach, changing the length and weights, sitting down and attempting a press. She offers you feedback at each stage.

When we want to learn something and we are alone or there is nobody round us with the relevant expertise, then the most basic approach to adopt is trial and error; discovery learning. When there is someone available who knows or can already do the thing in question, the most basic approach is imitation. You might repeat their words or copy their actions.

In the gym example, the trainer does not have to explicitly say 'copy me' or 'do this the way I am doing it', because we all implicitly understand that this is her intention. Imitation as a teaching strategy is ingrained in all of us. We have probably been teaching each other how to do things through demonstration and imitation way back into the evolutionary history of humans.

Copycats

The ubiquitous nature of the imitation teaching strategy leads us into error. Imitation works well for relatively simple tasks, but it is far less effective when the completed task is more complex and contains a hierarchy where one aspect of the performance depends on mastery of a different aspect. This is particularly acute for the complex products of human culture that we have not evolved to naturally acquire and that, as we saw in Chapter 1, are the stuff of the school curriculum.

By way of illustration, I think we might all agree that trying to copy the moves of a concert pianist would not be the most effective or efficient way of learning to play the piano. Instead, most piano teaching involves explicit instruction in musical notation, practising scales and other exercises, alongside a gradual increase in the complexity of pieces to be played. This is a bottom-up approach.

Yet, in education, we constantly reinvent the idea of learning a complex task by imitating the performance of experts – a top-down approach – because we somehow consider it to be more authentic. Practising discrete skills in isolation from the finished article is somehow seen as bogus and inauthentic, so we must start with a product firmly in mind. The product gives purpose to the learning.

In 1918, William Heard Kilpatrick, a progressivist educator and colleague of John Dewey, published his essay on 'The Project Method'. He was keen to highlight that he was not the first to make use of the idea of teaching through project work: 'At the outset it is probably wise to caution the reader against expecting any great amount of novelty in the idea here presented.' And project work will indeed seem familiar to anyone involved in education. To Kilpatrick, the key feature of a project is that it is 'purposeful':

> Suppose a girl has made a dress. If she did in hearty fashion purpose to make the dress, if she planned it, if she made it herself, then I should say the instance is that of a typical project. We have in it a wholehearted purposeful act carried on amid social surroundings. That the dressmaking was purposeful is clear; and the purpose once formed dominated each succeeding step in the process and gave unity to the whole. That the girl was wholehearted in the work was assured in the illustration. That the activity proceeded in a social environment is clear; other girls at least are to see the dress.

However, in order to actually complete such a task, it would need to be broken down into smaller components. If the girl cannot sew, then she would need to learn. She would also need to know how to cut and measure cloth and various techniques of dressmaking. Very soon, the purposeful act will disappear over the horizon. The scale of the task could become disheartening once she realises how far she is from actually making the dress.

Of course, this argument assumes that the girl is going to make the dress *properly*. Fixation on not letting a whole project slide over the horizon can lead to some strange teaching decisions. I remember completing a similar task at school with the key difference that we made the dresses out of garbage bags and sticky tape. This way, it was possible for a group of sardonic 14-year-old boys to produce an entire garment without all that tedious business of learning how to sew.

I am not a fan of Sir Ken Robinson and his celebrated 2006 TED Talk, *Do Schools Kill Creativity?*, but there is one small aspect which I cannot fault. In addressing the titular question, Robinson finds it necessary to define creativity, which he does as 'the process of having original ideas that have value'. Original ideas are not enough: *they must have value*. The clothes we made out of garbage bags were garbage. According to Robinson's definition and whatever the intent of the teacher, we had not been creative.

Ideas similar to Kilpatrick's project method are often touted as the latest innovative practices in education under names such as, 'project-based learning' (Vega, 2012) and 'the maker movement' (Flanagan, 2015). Writing on the Californian 'Mind/Shift' education blog, Thomas Markham (2015) echoes Kilpatrick's sentiments about purposefulness in emphasising projects 'that matter':

> To get at the depth of purpose and engagement necessary for learners today, there's work to do in PBL [project-based learning]. The way out of the box is to encourage teachers to let go, take risks, live with uncertain outcomes—and design projects that matter. Enter the world as it is at this time—as a place of wide open spaces and immense needs. Invent and deliver projects that retain the full power of PBL and, in the process, push education forward to meet its mid-century destiny.

Let's return to Kilpatrick's dressmaking example and ask what an alternative, bottom-up approach to teaching such a set of skills might look like: it would teach dressmaking skills discretely and individually, setting smaller, more immediate objectives. For instance, an initial aim might be to practise sewing to the point where the student can produce a line of evenly spaced stitches or, if using a sewing machine, can produce a straight line of stitching. The student may then perhaps make a simple pin-cushion or a purse where they would be shown how to measure and cut the cloth.

The top-down approach persists because people think that authentic, real-world projects will be motivating and because teachers routinely underestimate what is required to complete a complex task because they are suffering from the curse of knowledge.

Ambitious teaching

At least in the case of dress-making, many of the skills required for an expert performance are manifest and observable: we may see if a student cannot sew or cut the cloth straight and this may force a rethink. Yet many of the skills associated with expert performance in academic subjects are cognitive skills that are *latent*; they cannot be directly observed because they involve stuff that is going on inside the mind. And this means they are often neglected.

An interesting study by Major et al. (2016) illustrates a number of key features of contemporary education research. The study addresses the question of the extent to which teachers make use of 'ambitious' teaching. Note that it is not an investigation into whether such teaching is effective – that is assumed from the outset:

> We analyse teachers' attempts to change their approach, from traditional or teacher-centred practice to the ambitious approach suggested . . . . It is important to note that when we refer to teacher-centred teaching this is more than simply chalk, talk and textbook exercises. While such lessons might include group-work and investigations, the feature that makes them teacher-centred is that the teacher attempts to reduce the cognitive demand in the lesson so that students can progress easily through the tasks. In contrast, the aim of the [ambitious teaching] tasks is to offer higher levels of demand so that students have to think deeply about the mathematics and, as such, we characterise this as student-centred. [Reference removed.]

The traditional teachers presumably reduce the cognitive demand by breaking problem-solving tasks down into smaller components and then training students in these components in turn. Given that this is Grade 12 mathematics, mastering these components will be challenging enough for most students. Yet a teacher will not be as clearly confronted by a particular student's lack of mastery of one of these components as they would be by a child who cannot sew. To Major et al. (2016), ambitious teaching requires students to use 'their powers of reasoning and problem-solving'. In other words, with the components obscured, we may reify, or make concrete, abstract concepts such as reasoning and problem-solving and claim that students need to be exposed to more of *those* in order to think deeply. It is assumed that students are able to improve their problem-solving ability by doing more problem-solving – there is no need to break complex problems down into smaller components with reduced cognitive demand.

This call for reduced guidance clearly goes against most teachers' craft knowledge, which is why Major et al. struggled to convince experienced professionals to teach in this way. And yet it is a constant call. In an influential 2010 TED talk, speaker and former teacher, Dan Meyer, discusses a question from a textbook:

> Notice, first of all here, that you have exactly three pieces of information there, each of which will figure into a formula somewhere, eventually, which the student will then compute. I believe in real life. And ask yourself, what problem have you solved, ever, that was worth solving where you knew all of the given information in advance; where you didn't have a surplus of information and you had to filter it out, or you didn't have sufficient information and had to go find some. I'm sure we all agree that no problem worth solving is like that. And the textbook, I think, knows how it's hamstringing students because, watch this, this is the practice problem set. When it comes time to do the actual problem set, we have problems like this right here where we're just swapping out numbers and tweaking the context a little bit. And if the student still doesn't recognize the stamp this was moulded from, it helpfully explains to you what sample problem you can return to find the formula.

In the name of representing real life, we must ask students to solve complex problems from the outset, in the way that experts are able to do.

Perhaps an illustrative example of this approach is the 'Mantle of the Expert'. Pioneered by Dorothy Heathcote in the 1970s and still in use today, this drama-based teaching method endows students with notional expertise and then guides them using discovery learning techniques. As Heathcote and Herbert (1985) explain:

> Placing students in the position of being experts involves changes in the classroom communication system. A teacher cannot presume to give direct information to experts but instead

must set up ways in which the experts will discover what they know while at the same time protecting them from the awareness that they do not as yet have this expertise. In other words, through structuring the teacher protects the student from the debilitating effects of ignorance . . . . The teacher enables the group to gain the expertise through the application of the dramatic imagination to whatever social reality is to be symbolically represented.

So, effective, explicit forms of instruction are deliberately avoided. An example of such a project is where:

the students are "endowed" with the expertise of historians/ anthropologists charged with the responsibility of creating a Bronze Age community while the teacher assumes the role of public servant acting as the liaison between "the experts" and the government and as general facilitator of the project.

So, we begin with a particular context, pretend the students are already experts in this context and ask them to behave as such, dropping hints here and there to keep them on the right track but without giving them 'direct information'. We start with the complex scenario rather than with defining the discrete knowledge and skills we intend the students to acquire.

Deeper objectives

At this point, it is worth making explicit an assumption that has been implicit throughout the discussion so far, that the purpose of completing a dressmaking project is to learn the skills of dressmaking, the purpose of learning the piano is to be able to play the piano well and the purpose of solving complex mathematical problems is to improve at such problem-solving. This seems obvious, but it is not entirely clear this is what is always intended. Recall the supposedly generic skills such as critical thinking that we met in Chapter 1. It might be that developing *these* skills is the aim of top-down instruction rather than teaching any specific body of knowledge or procedural skill. By giving students hard things to do, they may grow in their abilities to overcome difficulties or might learn generic problem-solving strategies that can be applied in a range of situations. When challenged on the lack of evidence supporting the use of top-down instruction, proponents will sometimes advance such a case, arguing that they seek to achieve aims that are different from those of traditional education.

In 2006, a seminal article was published in the journal *Educational Psychologist* by Paul Kirschner, John Sweller and Richard Clark. In the paper, Kirschner et al. (2006) draw on cognitive load theory to explain why enquiry learning, problem-based learning and other 'constructivist' approaches 'do not work'. Their paper set the cat among the pigeons. Three rebuttals were published in the same journal, followed by a response from the original authors. There was a debate held at the *American Educational Research Association* conference in 2007 and finally an edited book where the arguments of those on both sides of the debate were published (Tobias and Duffy, 2009). Sigmund Tobias, one of the editors of this book, concluded:

> A careful reading and re-reading of all the chapters in this book, and the related literature, has indicated to me that there is stimulating rhetoric for the constructivist position, but relatively little research supporting it.

In her rebuttal to the original Kirschner et al. paper, Deanna Kuhn (2007) mounts the following argument, clearly signalling that she does not share the instructional aims assumed by Kirschner et al. (2006):

> Prescriptions like those of Kirschner et al., regarding how best to inculcate knowledge will not suffice, nor even get us very far, if questions remain unresolved regarding what knowledge to teach or even whether to teach knowledge at all . . . . After examining possible alternatives, I make the case that the only defensible answer to the question of what we want schools to accomplish is that they should teach students to use their minds well, in school and beyond. The two broad sets of skills I identify as best serving this purpose are the skills of inquiry and the skills of argument. These skills are education for life, not simply for more school. They are essential preparation to equip a new generation to address the problems of the day. [References removed.]

The ability to solve a certain type of mathematical equation is an ability that is relatively straightforward to define and to measure. In contrast, a skill of 'inquiry' or 'argument' is far more nebulous. Perhaps we have simply conjured such skills into being, reified them. It is not even clear that the concept of an 'inquiry' represents the same things in different situations. And similar to other supposedly general-purpose skills when examined closely, it seems reasonable to suggest that in order to successfully enquire within a discipline, you need a great deal of knowledge relevant to that discipline (see, for example, the argument of Tricot and Sweller, 2014).

Imagine, for instance, a scientist who is conducting a scientific investigation. This is an 'inquiry' because there is a question to answer. Such a scientist will have a thorough knowledge of the theory surrounding her research – not only will she have gained many formal qualifications within her field, but it is standard practice to conduct a rigorous review of all the relevant literature prior to starting an investigation. She will probably have command of the experimental method and apparatus involved. If not, she is likely to first run a set of trials just to establish that the equipment works well and is properly calibrated. Even though she may not know the results of this investigation in advance, she is likely to know the results of similar experiments and have some notion of the likely outcome or, at minimum, a narrow field of possible outcomes. She will know what current theories might predict in the circumstances and she won't have to look any of this up; she will be able to quickly bring relevant information to mind and evaluate competing ideas. When she does need to look things up, it will be to confirm the exact wording of quotes or identify a source or check specific technical details.

Now imagine a student completing a scientific investigation in a school classroom. On what basis will she generate a hypothesis? In an ideal setting, she may perhaps conduct some detailed research in advance of the experiment so that she can at least bring this to bear on the problem. Put differently, it might be a good idea to learn lots of relevant science first, in which case the effectiveness of different methods of achieving this becomes important. In a school setting, however, acquiring an expert level of background knowledge is not usually a prerequisite for completing the investigation. Therefore, what aspects of the authentic, expert performance are we actually replicating here? The answer is that we are replicating all the relatively superficial aspects that don't require any particular expertise. We ask students to mimic the behaviours of professional scientists. We want them to look like they are doing what real scientists do. It is reminiscent of some ancient religious ritual in which donning a hat and coat adorned with feathers and dancing with bird-like movements of the legs and arms endows a believer with the spirit of a bird.

Learning a discipline is not the same as practising it

Paul Kirschner, co-author of the influential Kirschner et al. paper and professor at the Open University of the Netherlands, tackles this issue directly (Kirschner, 2009) and suggests that confusion arises because people assume that the best way of *learning* science must be the way that science is *done* by professional scientists. Yet these two issues are not the same:

> how to learn or be taught in a domain is quite different from how to perform or 'do' in a domain (i.e., learning science vs. doing science) . . . experimentation and discovery should be a part of any curriculum aimed at "producing" future scientists. But this does not mean that experimentation and discovery should also be the basis for curriculum organization and learning-environment design.

Indeed, when Taconis et al. (2001) analysed the available studies, they found that science teaching that focused on the structure and function of students' knowledge base was more effective at improving problem-solving skills than teaching that focused on practising problems or learning problem-solving strategies – top-down approaches similar to learning through scientific enquiry.

According to Kirschner (2009), modelling the teaching of science on the *doing* of science is flawed for two reasons. First, children are not simply small adults and many will not necessarily possess the right cognitive equipment. Second, 'learners or novices are not miniature professionals or experts. Experts not only know more and work faster than novices, they also deal differently with problems and solve them in different ways'. Experts in a particular skill or subject differ significantly from novices. This is not just on a simple graduated scale – there are key *qualitative* differences. There is a vast literature on expertise, but I shall use just one example to illustrate the point.

Chi et al. (1981) investigated the different ways in which experts and novices categorised physics problems. The experts were advanced physics PhD students and the novices were physics undergraduates. Both groups were given a set of physics problems and asked to group them into categories of their own choosing. The novices tended to categorise the problems based upon surface features. So, for instance, they would group together problems that all involved objects on slopes. The experts, on the other hand, grouped the problems according to general physics principles. For example, problems that could be solved by applying the law of the conservation of energy were classified together.

It is interesting to ponder how we could make the novices behave more like experts – what could we do to help them think like giants? Advising them to 'group the problems according to physics principles' would not be particularly helpful because, as novices, they don't yet know what these are. It's a bit like advising a failing stand-up comedian to 'be funnier'. On the other hand, we could systematically and explicitly teach students the relevant physics principles, give examples and non-examples, ask questions to clarify meanings, guide practice and finally assign independent practice. That might work a little better.

A model of the mind

A complementary way of viewing this problem is through the lens of cognitive load theory. Cognitive load theory was developed, in part, to account for phenomena such as the worked example effect that we met in Chapter 2 – the effect where novices tend to learn more from studying a solution rather than solving an equivalent problem.

In cognitive load theory, the mind is considered to be made of two main parts that are relevant to learning – working memory and long-term memory. This model is a simplification. We do not know where these components are located in the physical brain and researchers have suggested a variety of additional components to memory such as sensory memory. However, these additional components tend to be left out of the cognitive load theory model because they add little to its ability to make predictions about the results of experiments in instructional design. There is a common misconception that scientific theories are intended to fully and completely describe reality. They are not. The intention is to create models that can be tested against reality and these models may vary depending on which particular aspect of reality we are interested in.

Working memory is essentially the store of items that we are conscious of at any given time. It is severely constrained. Imagine, for instance, that I asked you to remember the six letters, 'VKJQRX' for the next 20 minutes. With effort, you could probably do this. Now imagine that I ask you to remember the twelve letters, 'SKWHDIENDHSY'. This would be pretty hard to do unless you were using some kind of special memory technique.

Now imagine that I asked you to remember a different set of twelve letters, 'HIPPOPOTAMUS'. Your chance of remembering these letters is dramatically improved because you have a concept of 'hippopotamus' that is stored in your long-term memory. Instead of twelve items to hold on to, we now have only one. This phenomenon is known as 'chunking' and it demonstrates that we can effortlessly call knowledge from our long-term memory into our working memory and manipulate it – the ease with which we can draw on this knowledge probably contributes to the curse of knowledge bias.

It was George Miller who in 1956 established that the number of discrete items – whether 'S' or 'K' or 'HIPPOPOTAMUS' – we can hold in short-term memory in simple experiments of this kind is about seven. It is now thought that the limit of working memory – conceived of as not simply retaining items for short periods of time but also processing them – is approximately four items (Cowan, 2001).

The above example illustrates the point that it is possible to overcome the severe limits of working memory by having sufficient reserves of knowledge to call upon from long-term memory. Even highly complex items can be drawn upon and manipulated in the working memory in this way. This is a feature of expertise within a discipline.

In cognitive load theory, instructional tasks are said to contain either 'intrinsic' or 'extrinsic' cognitive load. 'Cognitive load' is the number of items to be processed in working memory. It is intrinsic if it is necessary to perform the task and extrinsic if it is not. An example of extrinsic cognitive load would be redundant information presented in a mathematics problem that is not relevant to finding the solution. The decision as to whether cognitive load is intrinsic or extrinsic will also depend upon the aim of the instruction.

The worked example effect occurs because worked examples provide novices with a narrow focus. Worked examples reduce the number of items, intrinsic or extrinsic, that a novice could potentially pay attention to and therefore reduce the cognitive load of the problem. Rather than search through many possible solution pathways, learners have only to pay attention to features of a single pathway.

As we progress from novices to experts, this effect reverses (Kalyuga et al., 2003). Experts learn more from solving problems than studying worked examples because they already have maps of the solution methods available in long-term memory. By solving problems, relative experts now gain experience of different forms of the problem. It becomes appropriate to include redundant information – the stuff of real-world problems – so that relative experts may learn how to decide which points are salient and which are not. Relative experts have working memory capacity available to make these distinctions because they already have schemas in long-term memory for solving the different problem types.

The idea of learning a complex task by identifying the behaviours of experts and then imitating those behaviours is therefore flawed. We may notice that experts are 'resilient' but this may come from a long history of effort and progress within a discipline. Experts in one particular field may not display such resilience in other fields where they lack expertise, and there is no reason to think that we can teach such resilience in a top-down fashion. Throwing novice maths students into complex and challenging problems with the intention of making them more resilient is perhaps a flawed idea. The same argument applies to any other feature of expert performance.

Learning cognitively demanding knowledge and skills by mimicking the behaviour of experts is also fundamentally at odds with our cognitive architecture (Sweller and Sweller, 2006). We may have evolved ways for naturally learning the kinds of knowledge and skills it has been critical to acquire throughout our evolutionary history, such as our mother tongue or how to hunt, but new academic knowledge and skills need first to be processed in a general way by working memory, and so we need an incremental approach to complex learning rather than one that overloads working memory from the outset.

The limits of working memory initially seem like a bug in human cognition, but they may actually be a feature. Evolution has taught our mind that some things are necessary and important, so we learn these effortlessly. But how do we know which recent cultural innovations are necessary and important to learn? Without some protective mechanism, our long-term memories could fill with a random assortment of low-grade information. Instead, by carefully measuring out small doses of the new information to be attended to, and by then testing this for its usefulness, perhaps through how often we are required to retrieve it (see, for example, Karpicke, 2012), our minds ensure that they build schemas of the greatest possible utility. Usefulness is not, of course, the same as veracity. If, in a particular cultural context, it is advantageous for an individual to believe in space aliens with two heads who visit Earth every Tuesday afternoon to take tea with the Queen of England, then this belief could become embedded as a schema in long-term memory despite being bonkers.

The gift that keeps on giving

Regardless of the evidence from cognitive science and elsewhere, the case for top-down instruction has been constantly rearticulated since at least the time of progressivists such as William Heard Kilpatrick. In an example from 2014, Jo Boaler, a professor of mathematics education, makes the case for a change in the way that we teach maths. She reflects on chairing a recent PhD viva:

> The young woman defending her PhD that day paced the room, sharing conjectures and connecting different theories. The mathematics we saw was visual, creative and alive. Sadly, however, the approach of Maryam and her students is far removed from that taught in British classrooms, and it is this chasm that stands in the way of gender equity in maths in Britain, and of better maths education in general.

Yes, there is a chasm between school mathematics and the conjectures and theories pursued by those seeking a PhD in mathematics. However, this is a not a result of dull, unimaginative schoolteachers, it is a function of the human mind and the differences between experts and novices. I am not entirely clear why this would be a gender issue.

To return to the analogy of a concert pianist, it would seem absurd to suggest that simply having a go at playing the piano, imitating what a concert pianist does, would be a good route to expertise, even if we backed this claim with the vague appeal that it would help our piano students to think like a pianist. The absurdity arises from the fact that we can visualise the physical skill required in playing a complex piece in a way that we cannot visualise the latent cognitive skills involved in composing an essay or planning an experiment. Nevertheless, plinking about on keyboards with no real training in technique has become a staple of music teaching in some schools under the assumption that, although it will not deliver us concert pianists, it will develop other, more nebulous qualities.

Greek tragedy

When it comes to academic pursuits, it is critical to ask: what are these hidden subcomponents that need to be developed in order to deliver a relatively expert performance? Take, for example, a question on the 2018 VCE English examination sat by 18-year-olds in Victoria, Australia. Having read the play *Medea* by Euripides, they were asked to write an essay on the topic, "'Disloyalty is the greatest crime in this play.' Discuss."

First, they must be able to read. They must have the background knowledge to understand what they read and understand class discussions. They must read *Medea* and learn key facts and concepts related to it. They must also be able to write an essay. This will require them first to be able to form letters, write words and then write sentences. They will need to be able to structure these sentences into coherent paragraphs which they are then able to weave into a coherent essay. Perhaps more mundanely, they must be able to finish writing the essay in the time given, which will require a great deal of experience of writing.

Writing is perhaps an example of an area that we often attempt to teach in a top-down fashion. Primary school students write stories or recounts of what they did at the weekend. Standardised assessments require students to write coherent arguments, so students write these over and over again, and the teacher provides 'feedback' in the form of a written comment at the end of each piece. Such feedback cannot hope to be corrective to all the possible spelling errors, run-on sentences, misunderstandings of content, unsophisticated vocabulary use and so on that may be present in an extended piece of writing, so teachers often focus on just one or two points. We are saying to students, 'Do this complex task badly and then we will point out a couple of the ways in which you did it badly.'

It is as if a football coach eschewed all drills and exercises, and insisted on coaching football players by requiring them to play entire games of football, remaining silent as they do so and then, at the end of each game, giving each player a couple of handwritten sentences on how to improve for next time: 'What went well is that your passing was largely accurate. You should work on your tackling and your position on the park.'

There are alternative ways to teach writing that work from the bottom-up. One of these that aligns well with Rosenshine's *Principles of Instruction* is set out in a 2017 book, *The Writing Revolution* by Judith Hochman and Natalie Wexler. Hochman is an experienced principal who developed a method for teaching writing that starts at the sentence level before gradually building over a period of years to more extended forms of writing, allowing targeted and specific teacher intervention at each point.

Anecdotal support for a bottom-up approach to teaching writing may be found in the unlikely figure of Winston Churchill. In addition to being a problematic dead, White, European male, Churchill was known for having a way with words. To Churchill (2010), his skill with language was at least in part a result of his school days:

> by being so long in the lowest form I gained an immense advantage over the cleverer boys. They all went on to learn Latin and Greek and splendid things like that. But I was taught English. We were considered such dunces that we could learn only English. Mr. Somervell – a most delightful man, to whom my debt is great – was charged with the duty of teaching the stupidest boys the most disregarded thing – namely, to write mere English. He knew how to do it. He taught it as no one else has ever taught it. Mr. Somervell had a system of his own. He took a fairly long sentence and broke it up into its components by means of black, red, blue and green inks. Subject, verb, object: Relative Clauses, Conditional Clauses, Conjunctive and Disjunctive clauses. Each had its colour and its bracket. It was a kind of drill. We did it almost daily . . . . Thus I got into my bones the essential structure of the ordinary British sentence – which is a noble thing.

It is perhaps ironic to imagine the reaction to a proposal to teach English in such a way today. It would likely be met with implacable opposition from many teachers on the basis that it would stifle students' creativity and prevent them from finding their own voices.

The pivot point

Hochman's explicit approach to teaching writing begins to highlight an important pivot point between methods such as explicit teaching and less guided approaches such as enquiry learning. Whatever the level of guidance provided in an enquiry learning context, it is not going to be the same amount as that provided by explicit teaching because the goal of enquiry is for students to at least find something out for themselves. According to the Australian government's Department of Education, Skills and Employment (n.d.):

> Inquiry-based learning is an education approach that focuses on investigation and problem-solving. Inquiry-based learning is different from traditional approaches because it reverses the order of learning. Instead of presenting information, or 'the answer', up-front, teachers start with a range of scenarios, questions and problems for students to navigate.

In contrast with such an approach, explicit teaching does not simply provide 'the answer', it breaks the problem down into its components. This is the key pivot point between the two. Imagine a standard explanation of a concept. Enquiry learning will miss something out from that standard explanation whereas explicit teaching will add something to it.

Despite being aware of this theory, I still find myself learning more about it in practice. An example of this is the 'slow-motion problems' developed by my maths teaching colleague, Adelle Holmes (Ashman, 2018). After demonstrating a worked example in class, I had been routinely asking my Year 12 students to complete a three- or four-step problem on their mini whiteboards. During a discussion about the data from an assessment where Adelle's students had performed better than mine, it became clear that she was asking students to perform just the first step of the problem on their mini whiteboards and hold this aloft before she asked them to perform the second step. This enabled her to provide feedback and get students back on track if necessary before the second step. Adelle was breaking things down even further than me and it appeared that her students were, as a result, understanding the concepts better.

Naughty teachers

The above example perhaps illustrates a gap between theory and practice. Interestingly, as relative experts, teachers may need a form of enquiry learning in order to help them apply principles derived from cognitive science and other forms of relevant research to the classroom. It should also give us pause before we assume that professional development led by a non-practitioner, however knowledgeable, is enough to move teaching practice on its own. Instead, reformers need to enlist the active collusion of teachers if they are serious about change.

At the moment, the literature contains many studies such as the Major et al. study in which teachers subtly undermine the intended teaching reform, and perhaps this is yet another example of where top-down approaches founder but bottom-up approaches succeed. Researchers who approach teaching with a set of assumptions about what effective teaching should look like – whatever the level of justification – and try to co-opt teachers into the process of making their own teaching look more like this archetype are taking a top-down approach. They are focusing on the finished product and not the components that go into that product. This focus on surface features is what Thomas Good previously warned us about (see Chapter 2). There is no tick-list for signing off on effective teaching, whether explicit or otherwise.

By focusing on smaller concepts such as the limits on working memory and how a particular activity can be impacted by these limits, we may build a more bottom-up approach to educational reform. Teachers as relative experts do not necessarily need a script to work from – although a script will help ensure fidelity to the plan – they need to understand how theory and practice combine in the context of professional enquiry. Happily, technology such as social media seems to have catalysed this process. In the absence of any discernible organising structure, teachers are blogging, organising and attending conferences, reading books about teaching, writing books about teaching, and largely bypassing the traditional gatekeepers of educational knowledge along with the traditional preoccupations of those gatekeepers. One such preoccupation is with individual differences and the need for teachers to 'differentiate' to cater for these differences – a preoccupation worth a chapter in its own right.

References

Ashman, G. (2018, June) Slow motion problems: A teaching method I have learnt this year. (Blog post). *Filling The Pail*. Retrieved from: https://gregashman.wordpress.com/2018/06/23/slow-motion-problems-a-teaching-method-i-have-learnt-this-year/

Boaler, J. (2014) Britain's maths policy simply doesn't add up. *The Telegraph*. Retrieved from: www.telegraph.co.uk/education/educationnews/11031288/Britains-maths-policy-simply-doesnt-add-up.html

Chi, M.T., Feltovich, P.J. and Glaser, R. (1981) Categorization and representation of physics problems by experts and novices. *Cognitive Science*, 5(2): 121–52.

Churchill, W. (2010) *My Early Life: 1874–1904*. New York: Simon & Schuster.

Cowan, N. (2001) The magical number 4 in short-term memory: A reconsideration of mental storage capacity. *Behavioral and Brain Sciences*, 24(1): 87–114.

Department of Education, Skills and Employment (n.d.) Inquiry-based learning. Retrieved from: www.education.gov.au/national-stem-education-resources-toolkit/inquiry-based-learning

Flanagan, L. (2015) How turning math into a maker workshop can bring calculations to life. *MindShift*. Retrieved from: www.kqed.org/mindshift/42717/how-turning-math-into-a-maker-workshop-can-bring-calculations-to-life

Heathcote, D. and Herbert, P. (1985) A drama of learning: Mantle of the expert. *Theory into Practice*, 24(3): 173–80.

Hochman, J.C. and Wexler, N. (2017) *The Writing Revolution: A Guide to Advancing Thinking Through Writing in All Subjects and Grades*. San Francisco, CA: John Wiley & Sons.

Kalyuga, S., Ayres, P., Chandler, P. and Sweller, J. (2003) The expertise reversal effect. *Educational Psychologist*, 38(1): 23–31.

Karpicke, J.D. (2012) Retrieval-based learning: Active retrieval promotes meaningful learning. *Current Directions in Psychological Science*, 21(3): 157–63.

Kilpatrick, W. (1918) The project method. *The Teachers College Record*, 19(4): 319–35.

Kirschner, P.A. (2009) Epistemology or pedagogy, that is the question. In Tobias, S. and Duffy, T.M. (eds) *Constuctivist Instruction: Success or Failure?* New York: Routledge, pp. 144–57.

Kirschner, P.A., Sweller, J. and Clark, R.E. (2006) Why minimal guidance during instruction does not work: An analysis of the failure of constructivist, discovery, problem-based, experiential, and inquiry-based teaching. *Educational Psychologist*, 41(2): 75–86.

Kuhn, D. (2007) Is direct instruction an answer to the right question? *Educational Psychologist*, 42(2): 109–13.

Major, L., Watson, S. and Kimber, E. (2016) Teacher change in post-16 mathematics: a multiple case analysis of teachers in the Zone of Enactment. 13th International Congress on Mathematical Education, Hamburg, 24–31 July. doi.org/10.17863/CAM.34735

Markham, T. (2015) *How to Make Sure That Project-based Learning is Applied Well in Schools*. Retrieved from: http://ww2.kqed.org/mindshift/

Meyer, D. (2010, March) *Math Class Needs a Makeover*. (Video file). Retrieved from: www.ted.com/

Miller, G.A. (1956) The magical number seven, plus or minus two: some limits on our capacity for processing information. *Psychological Review*, 63(2): 81.

Robinson, K. (2006, February) *Do Schools Kills Creativity?* (Video file). Retrieved from: www.ted.com/talks/sir_ken_robinson_do_schools_ kill_creativity

Sweller, J. and Sweller, S. (2006) Natural information processing systems. *Evolutionary Psychology*, 4(1): 147470490600400135.

Taconis, R., Ferguson-Hessler, M.G. and Broekkamp, H. (2001) Teaching science problem solving: An overview of experimental work. *Journal of Research in Science Teaching*, 38(4): 442–68.

Tobias, S. and Duffy, T.M. (eds) (2009) *Constructivist Instruction: Success or Failure?* New York: Routledge.

Tricot, A. and Sweller, J. (2014) Domain-specific knowledge and why teaching generic skills does not work. *Educational Psychology Review*, 26(2): 265–83.

Vega, V. (2012) *Project-Based Learning Research Review: Best Practices Across Disciplines*. Retrieved from: www.edutopia.org/pbl-research-practices-disciplines

4

WHAT KIND OF MONSTER TREATS ALL CHILDREN THE SAME?

Key Points

- Teachers are commonly asked to 'differentiate' teaching.
- Differentiation is a vague and often even contradictory concept.
- Differentiation could potentially increase achievement gaps between students.
- Alternative, more specific, models are needed to deal with differences between students.

Introduction

How do students differ from one another and in what way does this matter? One source of guilt in my early teaching career was my profound failure to 'differentiate' properly. Differentiation is teacher jargon for treating children differently, depending upon their particular needs. It seems a no-brainer – an obviously good thing. To an extent, teachers would struggle *not* to differentiate. Which teacher would refuse to re-explain a concept when asked by a student in the class? Which teacher would insist that a student should sit in silence after successfully completing an activity and simply wait for everyone else to finish? However, differentiation has come to mean more than a principle and has been formalised in ways that are often at odds with the practicalities of teaching and may even harm student progress.

Tasks, outcomes and jigsaws

When I trained, I was given two basic models of differentiation: a teacher may either differentiate 'by outcome' or 'by task'. If you differentiated by outcome, then you basically gave all students the same task to complete, but you held differing expectations of what they would produce. For instance, you might expect a more sophisticated analysis of the relevant science in a scientific report produced by a more able student. Exactly what we might mean by a 'more able' student is an interesting point which we will return to below.

Differentiation by task was promoted as preferable. In this case, you would give students different tasks to complete according to their ability level or any special educational need that they may possess. The main implication for teachers of adopting such an approach is a large increase in the work a teacher needs to do to prepare a lesson. This was the kind of differentiation that I felt guilty about not doing regularly. I was spending enough time designing my lessons without having to then create three or four subtly different versions of every worksheet or activity. Notably, a couple of colleagues who were in my cohort of new teachers and who did try to adopt this form of differentiation for teaching languages left the teaching profession after a couple of years.

As I entered employment, I became aware of other forms of differentiation: a teacher may group students and give the different groups different tasks to complete. One option was a 'jigsaw' activity where each group researched a different aspect of a topic. Groups of less able students could then be given simpler concepts to research than groups of more able students, before all groups then fed back their half-formed ideas and misconceptions to the whole class. Alternatively, another option was to have mixed groups in which less able students were combined with more able students in an effort to leverage the more able students to assist with explaining the content. Not for the last time in this discussion, we see differentiation being the justification for completely contradictory practices – in this case, mixed-ability versus similar-ability groupings.

I even invented a wheeze that I rolled out whenever we were to be visited by Ofsted – the English schools inspectorate – that seemed to work well in the early 2000s. At that time, Ofsted would visit a school, observe lessons and give each lesson a score – a practice that is now widely recognised as invalid (see, for example, Coe, 2014). Inevitably, one of the boxes that inspectors sought to tick was differentiation, so we made this easy for them. We would hand the inspectors a lesson plan with a section on it labelled 'differentiation' that we would then fill in with 'by targeted questioning'. This meant that we would direct oral questions to particular individuals – basic factual recall for some, exposition of a concept for others. At the time, it seemed to work in getting us through the differentiation hoop without creating vast amounts of busywork for the teachers in my department.

The few times that I did try to implement a differentiation 'by task' or a grouping approach, I noticed a number of hazards. First, the students seemed well aware of who was being given the easier work to complete, and this could be difficult to negotiate. Sometimes I would have teaching assistants present and they would effectively simplify a task on behalf of the group of students they were working with, reducing the need for overtly different work, but in their absence, I resorted to giving some students 'Sheet A' and others 'Sheet B', which they then quickly compared.

Another issue that is familiar to anyone who has ever completed a group project is the problem of social loafing – the tendency for individuals to expend less effort when working in a group than when working on their own (Karau and Williams, 1993). In my experience, this was compounded by arranging mixed groupings because the student who was perceived as most able would end up doing the more complex tasks, leaving the least able student to maybe write the title on a poster in bubble writing. Such an environment can only serve to exacerbate any pre-existing differences in knowledge between the students. Again, this is another recurrent feature of differentiation.

Similar-ability groupings presented their own problems with groups of the least able students struggling to stay motivated and requiring a large amount of teacher input. The nature of the task they were given mattered a great deal because any effort that could be diverted away from dealing with challenging subject content and into issues of presentation *would* be diverted.

So far, we have dealt with differentiation as an attempt to deal with differing levels of ability, but what do we mean by this? Is ability a relatively fixed quality of an individual, roughly equivalent to general intelligence of the kind that may be discerned by an IQ test, or is it a provisional quality that is constantly under review as students learn new content and gain new skills? As a teacher, it seems far more useful to think of ability as provisional, but it is possible that some differentiation practices betray a fixed view and communicate that view to students.

Learning styles

Ability, provisional or otherwise, is not the only axis on which students are claimed to vary. One popular idea is that students have different 'learning styles', such as 'visual', 'auditory', 'kinesthetic' or 'verbal', and that we should differentiate our teaching to accommodate them (e.g. Subban, 2006; Algozzine and Anderson, 2007; Levy, 2008). If this idea is true, then it generates a testable prediction – if we seek to determine our students' learning styles and then teach them in a way that meshes with these styles, they should learn more, either because the style of presentation has a direct effect on their learning or because by accommodating their preferences, students find the teaching more motivating and this leads to enhanced learning.

Pashler et al. (2008) conducted a review of the literature, seeking evidence to support this 'meshing' hypothesis and found none. In some circumstances, they found results that flatly contradicted the meshing hypothesis. They conclude that:

> The contrast between the enormous popularity of the learning-styles approach within education and the lack of credible evidence for its utility is, in our opinion, striking and disturbing. If classification of students' learning styles has practical utility, it remains to be demonstrated.

The lack of evidence supporting the practice of teaching students according to their supposed learning styles is becoming better known among teachers thanks to the work of people like Cedar Riener and Daniel Willingham (2010). Nevertheless, there are those who still seek to hold on to the concept in some form (e.g. Tomlinson, 2010) and there is evidence that it has been taught as part of Australian teacher education courses until relatively recently (Ashman, 2016, 2017).

Around the world

Setting aside learning styles, the obvious problem that differentiation presents is in managing the process itself. We still place teachers in charge of around thirty students. At any given point in time, a teacher can either be interacting with the whole class – a fairly traditional, teacher-led approach – or they can be interacting with a smaller component of that class.

Imagine a one-hour lesson in which the students are placed into six groups with each group completing a different task. If the teacher interacts with each group in turn, then this leaves only ten minutes of teacher input for each group. Even so, such a calculation is far too optimistic. Time will be required to set up the lesson at the start and some of the teacher input will not be instructional but will be about classroom management. Experience suggests that in all but the most favourable of possible circumstances, there will need to be a great deal of teacher redirection across groups; they will need to halt their discussion with the butterflies to tell the tadpoles to get back to work.

So, we should see this as a trade-off. In return for work that is perhaps better tailored to individual students' needs – and we will return to this assumption below – students will receive far less direct teacher input.

To see if this is a good trade, we can perhaps look to a comparison between different educational systems. Since the advent of tests such as the Programme for International Student Assessment (PISA) and The Trends in International Mathematics and Science Study (TIMSS) – tests that compare the performance of students from different countries and jurisdictions – the top spots have been dominated by the Far East. While the most successful Western states such as Finland and Canada have seen declines since the introduction of these tests (Alphonson, 2013; Coughlan, 2015), East Asia has generally held steady.

There has therefore been some interest in investigating the differences in teaching – particularly the teaching of maths – between countries of East Asia and countries such as the US and the UK. Some argue that differences are largely cultural and there is evidence to support this point – East Asian cultures are said to particularly value educational performance and parents often pay for private tuition (Jerrim, 2015). However, other researchers have decided to look at differences in the classroom.

An investigation by Miao and Reynolds (2014) found evidence that is relevant to our discussion. In Chinese mathematics classrooms, whole-class interactive teaching was being used 72 per cent of the time, whereas in English classrooms it was 24 per cent. The imperative to differentiate work in England may contribute to these figures with students completing different tasks either individually or in groups.

This trend is also in evidence in an analysis that I produced. TALIS is an international survey of teaching and learning practices conducted by the Organisation for Economic Cooperation and Development (OECD) who also run the PISA tests. There is a question on the survey that asks teachers how often they give different work to the students who have difficulty learning and/or those who can advance faster. I decided to plot the percentage of teachers in each country who answered 'frequently' or 'in almost all lessons' against that country's 2012 PISA maths score. The results can be seen in Figure 4.1.

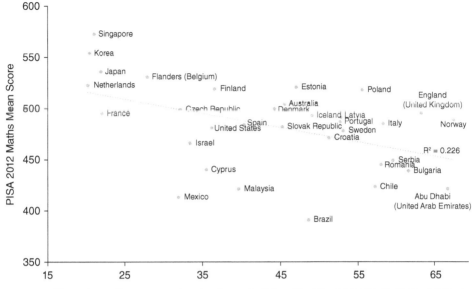

Figure 4.1   PISA data on teaching approaches

If anything, there is a slight negative correlation between the two, with the highest performing states using this kind of differentiation strategy the least. It certainly does not suggest that differentiation of this kind is associated with the education systems that tend to perform better on PISA.

The extent to which 'The teacher gives different work to classmates who have difficulties learning and/or to those who can advance faster' is also a question that the OECD asks students who are completing PISA assessments in order to calculate something described as the 'index of student-oriented instruction'. Researchers at PISA happen to believe that student-oriented instruction is good teaching because it is part of their definition (Echazarra et al., 2016): 'PISA defines the three dimensions of good teaching as: clear, well-structured classroom management; supportive, student-oriented classroom climate; and cognitive activation with challenging content.'

Unfortunately, analysis by Caro et al. (2016) of the 2012 PISA data shows that a student-oriented teaching strategy was negatively associated with mathematics scores in all of the 62 education systems investigated. Importantly, Caro et al. were able to look at the pattern within each country, so that their findings were not affected by differences between education systems.

Experimental evidence

So far, the evidence I have presented relating to differentiation has been correlational. Again, it could be that some other factor is causing the negative associations in PISA data. Perhaps there are systematic reasons why a student who struggles in, say, mathematics, is more likely to receive a form of differentiation. Or perhaps in the case of Caro et al., it is the other questions that make up the index of student-oriented instruction that are the main contributors to any effect. It is therefore worth looking at research that has attempted to directly measure the effect of differentiation through either a fully experimental or a quasi-experimental design.

One such study from the US (Brighton et al., 2005) sheds light on the issue of practicality. The primary aim was to evaluate the effectiveness of differentiated instruction (differentiation) when compared with other models in three different states:

> Participants in the study were assigned to either one of two experimental groups (Differentiated Instruction or Differentiated Authentic Assessment) or to a comparison group. Using a concurrent mixed method design, data were collected and analyzed relating to (a) the effects on teachers and students of a staff development program focusing on differentiated instruction, and (b) the effect on teachers and students of a staff development program focusing on differentiated authentic assessment strategies.

Unfortunately, the researchers effectively found few significant effects for differentiation on student achievement and the ones that they did find were largely weak effects. They concluded that this was due to teachers not implementing the model properly.

> Many aspects of differentiation of instruction and assessment (e.g., assigning different students different work, promoting greater student independence in the classroom) challenged teachers' beliefs about fairness, about equity, and about how classrooms should be organized to allow students to learn most effectively.

As a result, for most teachers, learning to differentiate entailed more than simply learning new practices. It required teachers to confront and dismantle their existing, persistent beliefs about teaching and learning, beliefs that were in large part shared and reinforced by other teachers, principals, parents, the community, and even students. The combination of the inherent complexity of differentiation with the ingrained nature of traditional deep structure beliefs about school often made encouraging large-scale changes in most teachers' practices difficult, if not impossible.

The 'complexity' referred to included the 'current realities of school such as large class sizes, limited resource materials, lack of planning time, lack of structures in place to allow collaboration with colleagues, and ever-increasing numbers of teacher responsibilities'. So, at the very best, we have a model that might work but is challenging for teachers to implement both for practical reasons and because it requires them to dismantle their existing beliefs. Is this likely to be an initiative that we could implement at scale and that would lead to long-term improvement?

A different study (Prast et al., 2018) sought to measure the effect of a teacher professional development programme about differentiation on the mathematics achievement of primary school students. The study lasted for two years and teachers were divided into three cohorts, one of which acted as a control group. The teachers in the first cohort were trained in differentiation in the first year of the study. Initially, the effects seemed positive with a small gain for students in this cohort compared to the other two. In the second year of the study, a second cohort of teachers were trained. However, the performance of students who had teachers in this cohort and in the cohort of teachers trained in the first year were not significantly different from each other or the control. The effect seems to have washed out over time. This is typical of the kind of effect we might see if people are initially enthusiastic about a new initiative, put in additional discretionary effort, but then fade in their enthusiasm as time passes. It therefore suggests little about the effect of the differentiation strategies themselves.

A randomised control trial investigating a financial literacy programme in the Netherlands also sheds light on two practices associated with differentiation (Iterbeke et al., 2019). Students were assigned to pairs either randomly or by matching their ability levels. In addition, the pairs were then further assigned to a condition where they either received 'uniform minimal instruction or differentiated instruction according to their ability level'.

The differentiated instruction consisted of materials with three different levels of guidance from minimal upwards. Perhaps surprisingly, the only significant effect found by the researchers across the conditions was differentiation enhanced learning for non-native students who were less proficient in the teaching language. Notice here that differentiation is not being compared with explicit teaching, but with an approach that provides minimal guidance.

We also need to bear in mind the nature of the comparison group when considering a randomised controlled trial that does appear to show a benefit for differentiation (Mastropieri et al., 2006). Initially, it appears that differentiated instruction was compared with 'teacher-directed instruction'. However, on further investigation, it becomes clear that students in both the teacher-directed instruction condition and the differentiation condition received the same teacher presentations. The difference was in the activity that students then undertook. Students in the teacher-directed instruction group completed fill-in-the-gap style worksheets independently, whereas those in the differentiation condition worked collaboratively in dyads selected so that students requiring assistance were paired with higher achieving partners. These dyads then completed a set of differentiated materials prepared for this purpose by the researchers, the level of which was decided by the teacher. Given that more than one factor varied between the control and experimental group, it is difficult to know what to conclude.

One approach to differentiation that is often promoted by researchers in known as 'Universal Design for Learning' or 'UDL'. For instance, in an article in *The Conversation* that attempts to explain differentiation, educational researchers Linda Graham and Kathy Cologon (2016) state that 'One particularly well-developed and internationally known resource is Universal Design for Learning (UDL)'.

At the time of writing, a visitor to the UDL website (Universal Design for Learning, n.d.) is confronted with three images of brains with different regions shaded in different colours. Until at least 2014, the main UDL website was asking readers to inform them about any evidence they found that supported the principles of UDL, turning the usual process of science – where we seek falsifying evidence – on its head (De Bruyckere, 2014). Neither sign is auspicious. When it comes to evidence of effectiveness, that is sadly lacking. A meta-analysis of available studies (Capp, 2017) found that 'The impact [of UDL] on educational outcomes has not been demonstrated'. In such circumstances, it is difficult to understand the enthusiasm for such an approach or why it would be recommended to teachers by academics.

The wide range of practices that may be described as different forms of differentiation give the concept a degree of 'fuzziness', in the words of a group of researchers from the University of Groningen in the Netherlands who sought to establish the effect of differentiation on primary mathematics performance by completing a systematic review of 21 studies that met their inclusion criteria (Deunk et al., 2018). Due to this lack of specificity, the effectiveness of differentiation is unclear, although their review did find small positive effects, especially when embedded in a computer-assisted environment or a whole-school reform. Such a qualification leads us to wonder, as with the old fairy-tale about the traveller who made soup out of a stone, what precisely was the key ingredient?

The basis for differentiation

It is not that individual differences are unimportant. To anyone who has ever taught, individual difference between students manifestly do matter. This is why individual tuition works so well, as demonstrated famously, if in rather contrived circumstances, by Benjamin Bloom (1984). The subtler point is that perhaps, in order to cater for individual differences in a classroom of thirty students, we end up throwing out something that is even more important: prolonged periods of interactive explicit instruction.

One largely unstated premise of differentiation is that it is *possible* for teachers to make accurate assessments of students' needs and then tailor their teaching accordingly. And yet we have seen with the example of learning styles that this may not always be the case. Those teachers who have drawn evidence from learning styles surveys to differentiate their lesson plans may have been convinced that they were engaged in a valid and worthwhile activity, but the evidence suggests otherwise. And learning styles may just be the tip of the iceberg.

Professor Robert Coe (2015) of Durham University's Centre for Evaluation and Monitoring suggests that teacher assessments tend to reinforce stereotypes and are biased against students with special educational needs, those with challenging behaviour, English language learners, those from low socioeconomic backgrounds and those with a personality different from that of the teacher. It is not hard to see the problem with differentiating work based upon such assessments.

Recall my 'differentiation by targeted questioning' strategy. How did I know who to target the questions to? How did I decide who got a factual recall question and who got a conceptual question? How did I know that the child who was asked a recall question could not have been capable of answering a conceptual question? Maybe, with the opportunity to discuss it with the person next to them, they might have been able to give it a go. I have perhaps placed an artificial limit on what this child can do. At the very least, they will not improve at answering conceptual questions if they are not asked such questions, so we have a mechanism for generating increased inequality within the class.

Now imagine that we are using a jigsaw task where different groups of students are given different things to do. Over time, we might see an increasing divergence between the students given the higher level tasks and the students given the lower level tasks. We might talk of the lower ability students as having a 'learning difficulty', yet we are partly responsible for creating and reinforcing this effect.

If this doesn't give enough cause for concern, then picture the child who is labelled as having a 'kinaesthetic' learning style. What might such a child be like? Given that the label is spurious, what factors will have led to them being assigned this grouping? It is interesting to note the findings of a 2004 study (Cooper et al., 2004) about White teachers' attitudes to aboriginal and non-aboriginal children learning mathematics:

> The most common perception was that Aboriginal students were *hands-on learners* in mathematics. Two teachers used the term *kinaesthetic* to describe the way in which Aboriginal students learn with one stating that *I have noticed with place value charts and things, making them touch, really made it sink in.*

This teacher suggested that the tactile nature of the way in which students learnt mathematics was not given enough consideration in the design of lessons. Another teacher stated the same position but in a negative manner, stating that Aboriginal students found pen and paper work difficult and had low tolerance for board work and copying information. ⌈Original emphasis.⌉

What kind of tasks will be assigned by teachers to children who attract the kinaesthetic label? From the above quotation, we can see that the avoidance of 'pen and paper' and board work are implied, yet these are at the heart of much academic learning. If these children are simply lacking the prerequisite skills, then avoiding these activities will not develop those skills. Again, we will see an increasing divergence between the haves and the have-nots.

Accommodate or address?

Such a discussion leads us to another junction where the imperative to differentiate could lead in two opposite and contradictory directions. Imagine we are presented with a primary school child who cannot read. As we have already seen, reading is fundamental to academic learning – the skill all others are built upon – and so reading failure is significant and profound. How may we differentiate for this child so that they may participate in a literacy lesson involving reading and discussing a story? One approach may be to *address* this need directly. The child could be the subject of an intensive, phonics-based literacy intervention. This could carry over into the lesson with the child being encouraged, perhaps with the support of a suitably trained teaching assistant, to sound out certain words in the story with the assistant helping with words beyond the student's current decoding ability. An alternative approach may be to *accommodate* the child's reading difficulty as a difference. Rather than being required to read the story, they may be given a pen that can turn text into audio or a teaching assistant may read the story in its entirety to them.

These two approaches come from a profoundly different place. One sees a deficit to be addressed, whereas the other sees a continuum of individual differences to be accommodated. Either stance may be appropriate in some circumstances. Some children may have diagnosed cognitive impairments that mean they will never be able to read, so enabling them to participate in the lesson by other means is equitable and humane. Some students may be subject to an intense intervention, but the decision may have been made not to carry that over into this particular literacy lesson, either to give them a break or because the content of the story is the critical learning intention and nothing should distract from that. For example, the story may illustrate a key safety issue such as potential stranger danger. Alternatively, the literacy lesson may be an entirely appropriate environment in which to continue a reading intervention. Lacking crucial contextual information, we do not have to come to any judgement. However, we should notice the fact that all of these nuanced and often conflicting approaches could be described as forms of differentiation, so the term loses any consistent meaning. Worse, it means opposite things. How can we know what a teacher or school leader means when they take to the lectern, clear their throat and exhort colleagues to differentiate more? What are they on about?

It is worth pausing at this point to note another set of factors that work in a similar way to each other and that also affect differentiation. The children most prone to the Dunning–Kruger effect (see Chapter 2) will be those with the least knowledge. Similarly, due to the curse of knowledge, teachers will struggle to notice this. A more knowledgeable student may notice that they do not understand something, seek clarification from the teacher and therefore receive instruction on this point. A less knowledgeable student will not realise that they need to do this and the teacher will not necessarily notice the problem, particularly if the student has been directed to activities that don't highlight it. Again, this cycle will act to increase the divergence between the two groups.

Ability grouping

This effect might explain what happens in ability grouping, yet another practice that *could* be described as a form of differentiation, although it is often extremely unpopular with differentiation advocates, as we will see. Ability grouping, setting or grouping for instruction is a common practice in many schools. For example, consider a school where three mathematics classes are scheduled at the same time and the students are then reorganised into a high-, medium- and low-ability class. This is not the same as 'tracking' or 'streaming' where the same students stay together across different subjects; instead, it is organised on a subject-by-subject basis and there is usually the scope for reorganisation between groups based upon new assessment information.

We might have two contradictory expectations of the effects of ability grouping. First, it is a way of tailoring the teaching more closely to the individual needs of the students but without the practical problems of organising different tasks within the one classroom. So, it should have a positive effect. On the other hand, we are creating a set of expectations and possible limitations by placing students in these groups. These may have a negative effect.

Logically, students in the low-ability group will actually need a more intensive course if they hope to close the gap with their peers. However, we may see more use of cutting-and-sticking and fewer pen-and-paper activities because the students are 'hands-on' learners. The children are likely to have had a frustrating history with the subject, which makes behaviour more difficult to manage, leading a teacher to assign tasks that children can do and enjoy rather than tasks that will challenge them. The group they are in then, to some extent, becomes their destiny.

It is also true that, due to such challenges, many teachers enjoy teaching the upper groups and don't enjoy teaching the lower groups. The lower groups would benefit most by being taught by the kind of experienced teachers who become heads of department, but heads of department are usually involved in allocating teachers to classes, so there is a potential conflict of interest here.

The research evidence on ability grouping is a little inconsistent (Kulik and Kulik, 1982; Slavin, 1990; Hattie, 2009), but it does seem to show a broad pattern where students in the upper groups tend to benefit, while students in the lower groups are sometimes disadvantaged. The overall effect comes out at close to zero in most studies. Depending upon your moral standpoint, you could therefore argue it either way: ability groups allow talented students to flourish or ability groups disadvantage the less able. I certainly think that a better shared understanding of the purpose of the lower groups would help – i.e. an intensive intervention focused on core academic skills and supported by strong behaviour management systems.

There is some evidence to support the idea that teachers may choose the wrong strategies for less able students. A US study (Morgan et al., 2015) found that first-grade maths teachers who had large numbers of students with mathematical difficulties in their classes were more likely to use manipulatives (plastic counting blocks and the like), calculators, music and movement. Yet the same study found that only teacher-directed instruction coupled with practice and drill was significantly correlated to achievement for these students.

A project conducted under the auspices of the UK's Education Endowment Foundation held out hope for resolving the question of ability grouping once and for all. The project, known as 'best practices in grouping students', aimed to avoid the pitfalls of previous research by conducting prospective studies in which the best possible versions of ability grouping and mixed-ability teaching were tested. For reasons that I do not fully understand, the best possible version of ability grouping was not compared directly with the best possible version of mixed-ability teaching. Instead, each of these methods was compared with control groups consisting of regular school grouping practices that would have included ability grouping and mixed-ability teaching. The trials suffered from recruitment and retention problems, and unsurprisingly, perhaps, neither study resulted in a positive effect for either of the two grouping practices (Roy et al., 2018a, b).

It seems like an opportunity missed. However, in a revealing twist, researchers associated with the project released a paper drawing from project data, arguing that ability grouping was a form of 'symbolic violence' (Archer et al., 2018). Having taken such an ideologically driven stance, it is hard to imagine how positive evidence for such a practice could have emerged from the project.

Whatever path we choose on grouping students, it is worth bearing in mind the cognitive science. We may perhaps be inclined to exaggerate the differences between individuals. This is possibly a part of our evolutionary heritage. But, as Dan Willingham and David Daniel (2012) suggest:

> when it comes to applying research to the classroom, it seems inadvisable to categorize students into more and more specialized groups on the basis of peripheral differences when education and cognitive sciences have made significant progress in describing the core competencies all students share.

Teachers can make great strides in improving student achievement by leveraging this body of research and teaching to commonalities, not differences.

This is a powerful message that strikes a humanist tone – our commonality as human beings is more significant than the many interesting differences between us.

Response to intervention

No matter the similarities between students, there are still obvious differences. Is there a way to deal with these differences in an educational setting without invoking the impracticalities, contradictions and unevidenced practices that constitute the bricolage of differentiation? Yes. It is known as 'Response to Intervention' (Fuchs and Fuchs, 2006).

Response to Intervention is a model that usually conceives of three layers of instruction. The first – 'Tier 1' – addresses all students in a whole-class context. 'Tier 2' is aimed at small groups of students who did not make sufficient progress in Tier 1. Finally, 'Tier 3' involved targeted, one-to-one intervention for those students who have still not progressed in Tier 2 (see Figure 4.2).

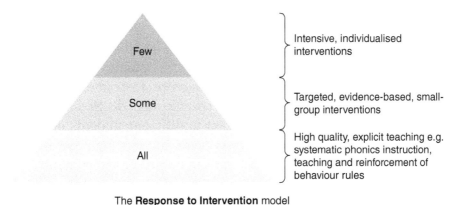

The **Response to Intervention** model

Figure 4.2 Response to Intervention

There are obvious advantages to Response to Intervention when compared to popular models of differentiation. All students will initially be given the same teaching, so teachers are not placed in the position of having to predict what individual students can cope with. In a differentiation setting, a student who struggles to add fractions may not be taught basic algebra, even though basic algebra may be something they get to grips with relatively easily, so an opportunity is lost. In Response to Intervention, all students will receive the same Tier 1 teaching.

And yet Response to Intervention is no panacea. It relies on three key ingredients that may not always be present. First, you need a high-quality Tier 1 approach. If you are teaching early reading and your Tier 1 approach is whole language or its ideological successor, balanced literacy, then you can expect a lot of students to arrive in your Tier 2 intervention. Second, you need valid screening assessments that will tell you whether a student has mastered the Tier 1 content or whether they need further intervention. Developing and deploying such screening assessments is no trivial matter. The political capital expended to introduce just one at a national level in the UK– the phonics screening check – was immense and a similar screen is the subject of ongoing debate in Australia as I write. Third, you need the organisational ability to provide the Tier 2 and 3 interventions. Where does the time come from for these interventions? How do you staff the small classes and individual support required?

Clearly, in almost all circumstances, the best Tier 1 approach will be some form of explicit teaching tailored to the content being taught, with Tiers 2 and 3 simply being more intensive, exhaustive versions of this.

Even if Response to Intervention presents logistical challenges, it perhaps gives us a guide as to a more systematic, well-defined approach to dealing with individual difference. Instead of relying on teacher perceptions, we screen for specific knowledge and skills. Instead of delivering different content to different students on what perhaps amounts to a fairly arbitrary basis, the starting point is that all students will have access to the same curriculum content. We move from an approach based on teacher judgements and the potential for bias to a more objective response.

Unfortunately, such considerations do not sit well with our contemporary individualistic, consumerist culture. What kind of monster wants to treat all students as if they are the same? What kind of monster would neglect to consider a child's burgeoning interest in super heroes and therefore fail to differentiate lesson content as a result?

But perhaps this is where the argument turns. Education is a community endeavour. There is such a thing as society, and education is an integral part of this. Proponents of differentiation may not realise that they are perpetuating individualistic, consumerist ideals, and perhaps when they realise they are perpetuating these ideals and why they are potentially harmful, they will begin to embrace an approach that sees education embodied in a knowledge-rich curriculum and enacted through explicit teaching as the birthright of every child.

Perhaps. But what about critical thinking, creativity and all that stuff that needs more than facts and procedures? Where does that come in? Let's find out.

References

Algozzine, B. and Anderson, K.M. (2007) Tips for teaching: Differentiating instruction to include all students. *Preventing School Failure: Alternative Education for Children and Youth*, 51(3): 49–54.

Alphonson, C. (2013) Canada's fall in math-education ranking sets off alarm bells. Retrieved from: www.theglobeandmail.com/news/national/education/canadas-fall-in-math-education-ranking-sets-off-red-flags/article15730663/

Archer, L., Francis, B., Miller, S., Taylor, B., Tereshchenko, A., Mazenod, A., Pepper, D. and Travers, M.C. (2018) The symbolic violence of setting: A Bourdieusian analysis of mixed methods data on secondary students' views about setting. *British Educational Research Journal*, 44(1): 119–40.

Ashman, G. (2016, February) Learning styles undead in Australian universities. (Blog post). *Filling The Pail*. Retrieved from: https://gregashman.wordpress.com/2016/02/20/leaning-styles-undead-in-australian-universities/

Ashman, G. (2017, January) Victoria University is still promoting learning styles. (Blog post). *Filling The Pail*. Retrieved from: https://gregashman.wordpress.com/2017/01/24/victoria-university-is-still-promoting-learning-styles/

Bloom, B.S. (1984) The 2 sigma problem: The search for methods of group instruction as effective as one-to-one tutoring. *Educational Researcher*, 13(6): 4–16.

Brighton, C.M., Hertberg, H.L., Moon, T.R., Tomlinson, C.A. and Callahan, C.M. (2005) *The Feasibility of High-end Learning in a Diverse Middle School*. National Research Center on the Gifted and Talented. Storrs, CT: University of Connecticut.

Capp, M.J. (2017) The effectiveness of universal design for learning: a meta-analysis of literature between 2013 and 2016. *International Journal of Inclusive Education*, 21(8): 791–807.

Caro, D.H., Lenkeit, J. and Kyriakides, L. (2016) Teaching strategies and differential effectiveness across learning contexts: Evidence from PISA 2012. *Studies in Educational Evaluation*, 49: 30–41.

Coe, R. (2014, January) Classroom observation: It's harder than you think. (Blog post). *CEMBlog*. Retrieved from: www.cem.org/blog/414/

Coe, R. (2015, April) Teacher assessment: Trust, precision, balance, quality – Part 3. (Video file). Retrieved from: https://vimeo.com/125186095

Cooper, T. J., Baturo, A.R., Warren, E., Catholic, A. and Doig, S.M. (2004) Young "white" teachers' perceptions of mathematics learning of aboriginal and non-aboriginal students in remote communities. In *Proceedings of the 28th Conference of the International Group for the Psychology of Mathematics Education*, Vol. 2, pp. 239–46.

Coughlan, S. (2015) Finns aren't what they used to be. *BBC News*. Retrieved from: www.bbc.com/

De Bruyckere, P. (2014, January) Does universal design for learning turn science upside down? (Blog post). *The Economy of Meaning*. Retrieved from: https://theeconomyofmeaning.com/2014/01/08/does-universal-design-for-learning-turns-science-upside-down/

Deunk, M.I., Smale-Jacobse, A.E., de Boer, H., Doolaard, S. and Bosker, R.J. (2018) Effective differentiation practices: A systematic review and meta-analysis of studies on the cognitive effects of differentiation practices in primary education. *Educational Research Review*, 24: 31–54.

Echazarra, A., Salinas, D., Méndez, I., Denis, V. and Rech, G. (2016) *How Teachers Teach and Students Learn: Successful Strategies for Schools*. OECD Education Working Paper No. 130. Paris: OECD.

Fuchs, D. and Fuchs, L.S. (2006) Introduction to response to intervention: What, why, and how valid is it? *Reading Research Quarterly*, 41(1): 93–9.

Graham, L. and Cologon, K. (2016) Explainer: What is differentiation and why is it poorly understood? *The Conversation*. Retrieved from: https://theconversation.com/explainer-what-is-differentiation-and-why-is-it-poorly-understood-55757

Hattie, J.A.C. (2009) *Visible Learning: A Synthesis of 800+ Meta-analyses on Achievement*. Abingdon: Routledge.

Iterbeke, K., De Witte, K., Declercq, K. and Schelfhout, W. (2019) The effect of ability matching and differentiated instruction in financial literacy education. Evidence from two randomised control trials. *Economics of Education Review*, 101949.

Jerrim, J. (2015) Why do East Asian children perform so well in PISA? An investigation of Western-born children of East Asian descent. *Oxford Review of Education*, 41(3): 310–33.

Karau, S.J. and Williams, K.D. (1993) Social loafing: A meta-analytic review and theoretical integration. *Journal of Personality and Social Psychology*, 65(4): 681.

Kulik, C.L.C. and Kulik, J.A. (1982). Effects of ability grouping on secondary school students: A meta-analysis of evaluation findings. *American Educational Research Journal*, 19(3): 415–28.

Levy, H.M. (2008) Meeting the needs of all students through differentiated instruction: Helping every child reach and exceed standards. *The Clearing House: A Journal of Educational Strategies, Issues and Ideas*, 81(4): 161–4.

Mastropieri, M.A., Scruggs, T.E., Norland, J.J., Berkeley, S., McDuffie, K., Tornquist, E.H. and Connors, N. (2006) Differentiated curriculum enhancement in inclusive middle school science: Effects on classroom and high-stakes tests. *The Journal of Special Education*, 40(3): 130–7.

Miao, Z. and Reynolds, D. (2014) How China teaches children maths so well. Retrieved from: https://theconversation.com/

Morgan, P.L., Farkas, G. and Maczuga, S. (2015) Which instructional practices most help first-grade students with and without mathematics difficulties? *Educational Evaluation and Policy Analysis*, 37(2): 184–205.

Pashler, H., McDaniel, M., Rohrer, D. and Bjork, R. (2008) Learning styles, concepts and evidence. *Psychological Science in the Public Interest*, 9(3): 105–19.

Prast, E.J., Van de Weijer-Bergsma, E., Kroesbergen, E.H. and Van Luit, J.E. (2018) Differentiated instruction in primary mathematics: Effects of teacher professional development on student achievement. *Learning and Instruction*, 54: 22–34.

Riener, C. and Willingham, D. (2010) The myth of learning styles. *Change: The Magazine of Higher Learning*, 42(5): 32–5.

Roy, P., Styles, B., Walker, M., Bradshaw, S., Nelson, J. and Kettlewell, K. (2018a) Best practice in grouping students intervention B: Mixed attainment grouping. *Education Endowment Foundation (EEF)*. Retrieved from: https://educationendowmentfoundation.org.uk/public/files/Projects/Evaluation_Reports/Intervention_B_-_Mixed_Attainment_Grouping.pdf

Roy, P., Styles, B., Walker, M., Morrison, J., Nelson, J. and Kettlewell, K. (2018b) Best practice in grouping students intervention A: Best practice in setting. *Education Endowment Foundation*. Retrieved from: https://educationendowmentfoundation.org.uk/public/files/Projects/Evaluation_Reports/Intervention_A_-_Best_Practice_in_Setting.pdf

Slavin, R.E. (1990) Achievement effects of ability grouping in secondary schools: A best-evidence synthesis. *Review of Educational Research*, 60(3): 471–99.

Subban, P. (2006) Differentiated instruction: A research basis. *International Education Journal*, 7(7): 935–47.

Tomlinson, C. (2010, June) Carol Ann Tomlinson on learning styles. (Blog post). *ASCD In Service*. Retrieved from: https://inservice.ascd.org/carol-ann-tomlinson-on-learning-styles/

Universal Design for Learning (n.d.) Retrieved from: www.cast.org/our-work/about-udl.html#.XsXw2WgzaUk

Willingham, D. and Daniel, D. (2012) Teaching to what students have in common. *Educational Leadership*, 69(5): 16–21.

5

THINKING OUTSIDE
THE BOX

Key Points

- We can view critical thinking and creativity as forms of problem-solving.
- There is no reason to think alternatives to explicit teaching are needed in order to develop problem-solving ability.
- If a strategy is applicable to a wide range of problems, it is likely to be less useful than a more specific strategy.
- Attempts to teach critical thinking as a generic skill are misguided.
- We must not confuse critical thinking with critical theory.

Introduction

Sometimes, people may agree that there is evidence that explicit teaching is effective for imparting content knowledge, but will maintain there are other goals of education and that these other goals are better met by other means. We have already discussed such arguments and the lack of evidence to support them, but the idea is a powerful one.

A current version centres on the skills that students will need in the future, an idea we met in Chapter 1. These supposed skills include the ability to think critically, communicate effectively, solve problems and collaborate with peers, and they are typically discussed as if they are generic in nature. Once you possess such a skill, you can apply it to pretty much anything. In a 2015 working paper for UNESCO, the United Nations cultural body, the perceived conflict between achieving these aims and explicit forms of teaching is made clear (Scott, 2015). Explicit teaching is characterised pejoratively as a 'transmission' model which, 'typically leads to indifference, apathy and for most learners, boredom'. Instead, 'Metacognitive development is . . . encouraged by problem-based learning activities that require peer collaboration', and so on.

A slightly different take on a similar theme is presented by Alice O'Keeffe in *The Guardian* (2020). According to O'Keeffe, 'traditional academic learning,' has had its day. In the future, students will need emotional intelligence and the ability to cope with uncertainty and rapid change. Such abilities 'are best fostered by an education system that prioritises . . . "the four Cs": critical thinking, communication, collaboration and creativity'.

In this chapter, we will see that, to the extent to which objectives such as developing critical thinking may be defined, explicit teaching, whether traditional or otherwise, is still the best bet.

Not winning Twitter

Twitter is an interesting microcosm in which to observe debate. The ground floor consists mainly of people insulting those they view as political opponents. However, if you hang around on the mezzanine level for long enough, you are likely to observe someone accusing another of propounding a logical fallacy.

Logical fallacies are interesting and they certainly do abound on Twitter and other social media forums. They are essentially bad arguments. Probably the most common is the *ad hominem* or personal attack. For instance, in response to Alice O'Keeffe, I may declare, 'Alice O'Keeffe is a literary critic and a journalist. She's not a teacher or educator. She doesn't know what she is on about!' Although true to an extent, such an argument has little bearing on whether O'Keeffe is right or wrong. It is quite possible for someone from outside a field to be right, just as it is quite possible for someone ensconced in a field to be wrong. Rather than dealing with the argument that has been put forward and the evidence to support or refute that argument, an *ad hominem* attack attempts to damage the credibility of the person making the argument.

Another common logical fallacy is the strawman. In this case, Person A advances an argument and Person B attacks something that is not quite the argument that Person A advanced. Person B is attacking a 'strawman' version of the argument because this is easier to do. For instance, I may argue for structured early reading lessons and an opponent may argue that I am wrong because play is important and children should be given the opportunity to play. I have never argued they should not be allowed to play.

And this example is also an example of the false choice fallacy. A false choice is where we are presented with only two options when others are available. In this case, we are presented with the option that children may have structured reading lessons or they may be able to play, but we are not presented with the possibility that they may be able to do both at different times – that possibility has been fallaciously excluded.

Paul Graham, a computer scientist and entrepreneur, wrote an influential 2008 Web essay on internet disagreements in which he argued that we would all be happier if we could lay off the fallacies. Once we focus on rebutting the main idea of an argument rather than attacking the person advancing it or an unfair characterisation of their argument, people are less likely to feel personally affronted and we may all edge ever closer to the elusive truth.

Stepping back a little, perhaps the ability to spot logical fallacies is a generally applicable critical thinking skill of the kind that critical thinking advocates are keen to advance. Logical fallacies may be found in *any* field of knowledge and if we are educated about them, perhaps we can spot them in any field of knowledge. If we teach students about logical fallacies, they will be able to see them in the media and perhaps be less likely to fall for bad arguments or use fallacious reasoning themselves. They may even live happier intellectual lives as a result. That would be powerful indeed.

And yet logical fallacies may not be exactly what the futurists are looking for. On examination, they look a lot like knowledge – you need to know what the fallacies are called and what they look like. This would seem well suited to an explicit teaching approach where the fallacies are first explained, one at a time, with students given plenty of worked examples and practice problems, before they are gradually interleaved, requiring students to identify examples of each fallacy, and so on. The research on problem-based learning versus explicit teaching approaches cited by Kirschner et al. (2006), for example, would be directly relevant. But we have at least found something that is generally applicable and not bound up with specific subject knowledge, haven't we? Well, sort of.

Despite their wide deployment, the identification of logical fallacies is rarely a *coup de grace* on Twitter. The reason is perhaps ironic – logical fallacies do not address the substance of an argument, only its form. I could advance an argument completely absent of logical fallacies and be wrong. The Ptolemaic model of the universe, for instance, with the Earth at the centre and celestial bodies revolving around it on the inside of different spheres, complete with epicycles for planets, is a logically consistent system. It's still wrong. How do we know? We have evidence specific to planetary motion.

Similarly, if you were interacting with an anonymous Twitter account called 'King Butthead' and that account claimed that 5G internet masts cause viral diseases, you might suggest, 'I do not believe you – you're just an anonymous Twitter account with a silly name who doesn't have any understanding of science.' Technically, this is an *ad hominem* fallacy, but I would hardly blame you for your reaction. It would seem pretty reasonable to me. Yes, formally, the fact that King Butthead is anonymous and we cannot check his credentials does not *necessarily* mean that he is wrong, just as the fact that if someone is a professor of virology that does not *necessarily* mean they are right. However, logical fallacies often apply only to formal deductive logic. Other forms of logic are available such as inductive logic. This is the kind of logic used by scientists and involves making claims based on probabilities rather than absolutes. In the case of King Butthead, an assessment of the probability of him being right does not work in his favour. Of course, anyone with a modicum of scientific knowledge can evaluate the substance of the claim directly and find it to be absurd. So, there is a trade-off. Although widely applicable, logical fallacies are no substitute for relevant subject knowledge.

Even so, I cannot help thinking it would be good if educationalists were a little more familiar with the concept of the burden of proof – that the person who makes a claim has the duty to provide evidence for it and it is not the duty of others to find evidence to disprove it. Shifting the burden of proof on to others is therefore fallacious. If this was better understood, we may find fewer claims made about generic twentieth-century skills and the best ways to teach them.

Useful versus general

Whenever we find a candidate for a generic ability, we are likely to be confronted with a situation similar to that involving logical fallacies. There seems to be a trade-off. The more useful the ability appears to be, the more specific it is to a particular subject area. The more generally applicable an ability is, the less useful it seems to be and will pretty much always be bettered by knowledge relevant to the specific situation.

For example, one proposed critical thinking ability is to be able to look at an argument from multiple perspectives. However, as Dan Willingham has written (2007):

> if you remind a student to 'look at an issue from multiple perspectives' often enough, he will learn that he ought to do so, but if he doesn't know much about an issue, he can't think about it from multiple perspectives.

I would add that if you *do* know enough to think about an issue from multiple perspectives, you are probably doing so already. So, perhaps these abilities exist on a continuum that recognises the trade-offs involved (Figure 5.1):

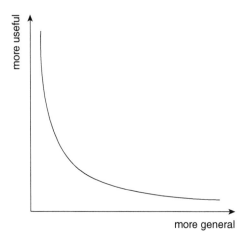

Figure 5.1 Useful versus general abilities shown as a trend

However, even if abilities do exist on a continuum of this kind, then they are unlikely to all fit neatly on the line. Clearly some, such as the ability to identify logical fallacies, will have a greater combined amount of both usefulness and generalness. So, Figure 5.2 may be a better representation of exactly what is going on:

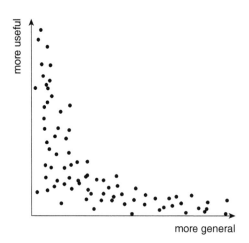

Figure 5.2 Useful versus general abilities shown individually

Considering abilities in this way has value to teachers when designing a curriculum because we can look for those that have the greatest combined usefulness and generalness and make them a priority for instruction. An understanding of the theory of evolution, which cuts across so many areas of biological science and beyond, would be one candidate. Linear equations, useful across the sciences and even the humanities, may be another. Understanding how to structure a critical essay will have benefits across the arts.

However, these are not the kinds of things people tend to be talking about when they discuss the need to develop critical thinking skills. What might those abilities look like?

Skilful thinking

In their 2010 book, *Thinking-Based Learning: Promoting Quality Student Achievement in the 21st Century*, Swartz et al. give a typical, if a little grandiose, rationale for teaching critical thinking skills.

> A presidential commission concluded that various U.S. intelligence agencies failed to validate the reliability of their sources in assessing prewar conditions and events in Iraq. The reference, of course, is to those alleged 'weapons of mass destruction' that served as the pretext for going to war in Iraq. Skillful thinking about the reliability of these sources could have avoided these problems, and yet some of the most important role models in the United States failed to exhibit such thinking. It is our contention that skillful thinking can and should be taught to students in our classrooms at every level.

They define 'skillful thinking' as 'the proficient and strategic application of appropriate thinking skills and productive habits of mind, as needed, to develop thoughtful products, such as decisions, arguments, and other analytical, creative, or critical products'. This is extremely broad.

It is easy to make fun of such a project. What kind of learning is not 'thinking-based', for instance? And the book proceeds through sequences of all-encompassing generalities, rendering it unfalsifiable in the style of those business and self-help books that exhort us to stick to our guns, apart from at those times when it is necessary to compromise.

Nevertheless, books and articles on the subject of critical thinking skills abound. Possibly the best known resource of all is the Visible Thinking programme created by Project Zero at Harvard Graduate School of Education. Visible Thinking aims to integrate various thinking routines into content learning (Ritchhart and Perkins, 2008) such as 'connect–extend–challenge', which aims to help students make connections.

Are there grounds to be optimistic about such approaches? Well, they do offer new and interesting ways for students to interact with content, and so may potentially improve classroom instruction if they lead to better retention of, and ability to apply, that content. But are they really improving the quality of students' thinking in a more general sense? Perhaps not.

Carl Bereiter, a researcher who we met when discussing Project Follow Through, develops an extended argument about the various strategies that have been proposed to improve thinking in a chapter titled, *Critical Thinking, Creativity, and Other Virtues* from his 2002 book, *Education and Mind in the Knowledge Age*. It is a short and devastating survey of the landscape.

First, he notes that he does not intend to review all thinking skills programmes. They are often integrated as part of some other curriculum and therefore it can be hard to tease out the effects. When the effects are measured, the measures often contain the same assumptions underpinning the intervention and do not demonstrate transfer to useful abilities in the real world. Transfer is the ability to apply what we have learnt in one context to a similar problem in a different context. Transfer, particularly 'far' transfer to different fields of knowledge, is notoriously difficult to achieve in educational research (see, for example, Sala and Gobet, 2017) and this alone should cause us to pause before we assume the existence of generic capabilities.

Bereiter reviews a number of approaches that have been pursued to develop better thinkers, including those that directly attempt to physically improve the brain, cognitive skills training and thinking strategy instruction. He finds little strong evidence to support any of them and makes the key point that when you analyse expert thinking by asking experts to think aloud as they perform a complex task, the actual thinking they perform bears little relationship to the kinds of strategies thinking skills programmes teach to students.

However, Bereiter's strongest criticism is for those advocates of critical thinking skills who fail to think critically about the prospect of teaching them. Their sheer credulity bothers him. He likens the exhortation to 'teach students to think' to one to 'teach students to digest' and complains:

Teaching thinking is treated as a straightforward matter like teaching furniture refinishing. It does not occur to people to question whether a course that claims to teach it actually does so. Heeding the analogy to teaching digestion, I do not find it obvious that thinking is teachable at all or, indeed, what it would mean to teach thinking.

In the intervening years since the publication of *Education and Mind in the Knowledge Age*, little new evidence has emerged to support the approaches to teaching thinking that Bereiter analysed. Moreover, recent studies seem to have further confirmed some of his conclusions. For instance, see Melby-Lervåg et al. (2016) on the lack of evidence for working memory training.

If we turn the telescope around and look through the other end, a different question arises. The world has not, historically, been short of good thinkers. In the absence of courses in critical thinking skills, how did they learn how to think? After all, critical thinking may be dubbed a notional twenty-first century skill but it has come in rather handy in a least a few of the centuries prior to that.

One potential answer is that critical thinking abilities do indeed emerge as a result of more traditional forms of education, but that these forms of education are not optimal for developing such abilities. If we instead adopted a curriculum that paid more heed to the development of critical thinking skills, we may find that a greater number of students are able to think critically and to a greater depth.

We are now in possession of an empirical question. We can potentially test whether exposure to critical thinking skills training results in a greater development of these capacities than a more traditional alternative. Nevertheless, it is a difficult empirical question to address. It would be challenging to chart improvements in macro-abilities such as critical thinking over a short time-frame without producing trivial and debatable results. You could imagine, for instance, teaching students to check the sources of internet articles and then test whether they were more inclined to do this on a subsequent assessment than students in a control group who had not been taught to check the sources of internet articles. I do not think we would need to conduct any such experiment because we could be reasonably confident that the results would likely favour the intervention. However, I doubt whether many of us would then confidently claim that we had improved the students' critical thinking skills in any meaningful sense.

Instead, we would need to take a longer term view and longitudinal research of this kind tends to be scarce. It also tends to be correlational, with long-term true experiments being extremely rare. Nevertheless, if we expect training in critical thinking skills to have an educationally meaningful effect, then, over the long term, we should see a positive relationship between such training and improvements in tasks that require critical thinking.

A 2016 meta-analysis by Huber and Kuncel sheds some light on how critical thinking is affected by a university education. The good news is that critical thinking abilities are generally improved by a college education. As the authors state, 'college appears to produce critical thinkers about as well as motivation produces good students'. Employers seeking graduates are therefore not doing so in vain and students may have a reason to pay their tuition fees. Unfortunately, whether students study discrete courses in critical thinking skills or not during their time at university made little difference to the gains in critical thinking abilities.

If teaching critical thinking skills was so effective, would we not see a signature of that by now? On the other hand, if it is not the right approach to improving critical thinking abilities, then what is? One possible conclusion is that if critical thinking is improved by a university education, regardless of whether that education includes specific training in critical thinking, there is something else at work. That something else may be a wider and deeper understanding of the world and critical thinking might emerge out of that.

The surfing mind

According to cognitive load theory, there are only two ways we may gain new knowledge of the world. The first is from other people, and we are pretty well adapted for acquiring it in this way. The second is via randomly generating problem-solving steps and testing them against reality (Sweller et al., 2011). If true, this assumption alone perhaps explains the efficiency of explicit teaching.

In the cognitive load theory argument, problem-solving is being used in the widest possible sense. A problem could be to discover a new fact, evaluate the veracity of a source or perhaps develop a novel product that has value. These are schematically similar and so problem-solving, critical thinking and creativity, although differing greatly in detail, draw upon the same set of processes at the abstract level. Knowledge is also defined in the broadest possible sense – it includes empirically verifiable facts about the world but also beliefs – and even entire systems of beliefs – that may be empirically false. 'Dolores thinks Dan is cheating on her' is knowledge that could be obtained from another person or by random guess-and-check regardless of whether the mark on Dan's collar is actually lipstick or ketchup.

At first, the idea that we either obtain knowledge from someone else or we use a random guessing procedure seems deeply counterintuitive. Surely the guesses made by experts are going to be better than those made by novices. Yes, but that's because knowledge does not come in discrete, independent lumps, but in hierarchies and arrangements. An expert's knowledge takes them much further than a novice. When experts start guessing, they do so from a vantage point that is much closer to the solution.

Figure 5.3 represents an individual with relatively little knowledge relevant to the problem. They cannot surf very close to the solution and must start guessing at an earlier point. The number of directions they may then take makes it improbable, but not impossible, for them to alight on the goal state.

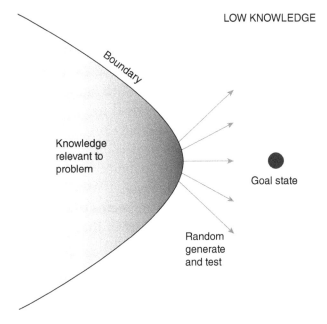

Figure 5.3 Low knowledge individual

In contrast, Figure 5.4 represents a high knowledge individual. This could, perhaps, be the scientist referred to earlier who is conducting an experiment, knows the relevant theories, knows the results of similar experiments and makes a valid prediction about what may happen. The high knowledge individual is far more likely to achieve the goal state.

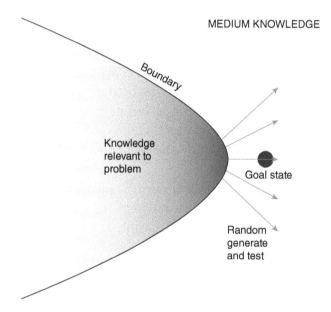

Figure 5.4   High knowledge individual

Finally, Figure 5.5 represents an individual who already possesses knowledge of how to solve the problem. Such knowledge will be practical as well as declarative – the individual has solved problems like this in the past. This knowledge could have originated from previous random guess-and-check activities or it could have been communicated from another individual. For instance, the problem could be driving to work or cooking a simple meal.

The argument about critical thinking seems to stem from a lack of recognition that these three state as part of the same continuum. If we conceptualise problem-solving, critical thinking or creativity as different in nature from solving problems you already know how to solve, then we see them as requiring different teaching methods. In the future, humans will be needed to solve the kind of non-routine problems that computers cannot solve, the thinking goes, and so

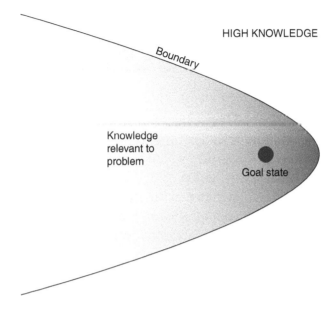

Figure 5.5 Individual who is already capable of solving the problem

instead of teaching them content knowledge, we need to teach them how to think critically. However, content knowledge is what helps us surf ever closer to our goals.

If I wish to compose a concerto, there is a chance that I will sit down at a piano and, with a suitable amount of trial and error, develop a passable piece. However, if I have plenty of training in piano, both practical and theory, have composed smaller pieces, have played and am familiar with many other concertos, I have a better chance.

Human nature perhaps stands in the way of us grasping this. When presented with an exceptional performance that we cannot fathom, it is perhaps instinctive to assume that the individual concerned has some magical quality – a genius – that sets them apart from mere mortals. And yet studies of expertise consistently show the sheer quantity of deliberate practice that goes into the making of an expert (Ericsson, 2008).

Consider a stage magician. When we see something amazing – a destroyed playing card appearing in a pocket or a person seemingly teleported from the stage into the audience – we know that what we are witnessing is the result of many hours of gruelling practice. But we still want to believe in the magic. We still want to believe in the person with spooky powers. Stage magicians are experts and experts are stage magicians. Like Newton, they are all standing on the shoulders of giants. But perhaps they are not all as grumpy as Newton.

On being grumpy

Isaac Newton was famously grumpy. It is hard to be sure at such a distance just exactly how grumpy Newton was, but he was accused of vindictiveness by his peers and even of making up conversations that never happened. He quarrelled with Robert Hooke over who first developed similar ideas about optics and he quarrelled with Gottfried Leibniz about which of them invented calculus. He quarrelled with John Flamsteed, the first Astronomer Royal, who felt his assistance in providing Newton with astronomical observations had not received proper acknowledgement. In short, and despite his protestations of dislike for disputes, Newton appears to have been decidedly quarrelsome (Keynes, 1995).

Personality research has coalesced around the idea that there are five main personality traits. These 'Big Five' are neuroticism, extraversion, openness to experience, agreeableness and conscientiousness. Some people are highly agreeable and tend to be cooperative with those around them; others are not. These personality traits seem to stay pretty stable over time (Soldz and Vaillant, 1999; Cobb-Clark and Schurer, 2012), although in the case of traits such as neuroticism, there is some evidence of a response to interventions such as psychotherapy with particular groups of individuals and for specific issues such as anxiety (e.g. Weitz et al., 2018).

It is certainly plausible that personality traits affect abilities such as problem-solving, critical thinking and creativity. Those who are highly agreeable may find it harder to challenge widely held opinions. Those who, like Newton, are a little less agreeable may find this easier to do. Thinking outside the box might be easier if you are not socially or emotionally invested in the box, and perhaps significantly enhanced if you are motivated to smash the box to pieces.

Yet given the relative stability of personality traits and the fact that teachers are not trained psychotherapists, we may question whether the aim of adjusting students' personalities is realistic and viable. And that question only arises if we think that personality adjustment is the right thing to do.

If it were to be possible, what is the ethical position of personality adjustment? In a deep sense, we are attempting to change who a person is, and that should not be entered into lightly. Taking a more utilitarian stance, there is some evidence that the Big Five personality traits correlate with happiness, at least when measured using a survey instrument such as the Oxford Happiness Inventory (see, for example, Furnham and Petrides, 2003). If so, we have to wonder what effect a programme of personality adjustment optimised to increase critical thinking will have on other important aspects of well-being. Newton was a critical thinker, but was he happy? What matters more? Should teachers decide?

And yet personality may not be the only constraint on young people applying their knowledge in a critical way. Social structures could plausibly diminish critical thinking. In a rigidly hierarchical society where everyone obeys their parents or their bosses without question, we can imagine the stifling of critical thought. Similarly, the apparent effectiveness of explicit forms of teaching represents its own danger. What if we explicitly teach questionable assumptions and then rehearse the application of such assumptions over time?

In such a context, thinking routines may have a role. By modelling and then asking students to view an issue from multiple perspectives, we give permission for them to try a little critical thinking in a way they may otherwise not have encountered. In the safety of the school and provided we have sufficient societal consent, we can challenge some taboos. But we do not have to stop at thinking routines. The old favourite of asking students to write an essay arguing for a position they disagree with is a task of a similar kind.

Yet, such a project is fraught with danger, even in the world's liberal democracies where differences of opinion are theoretically able to coexist. Where we lack community consent, even if consent is issued by the broader society, teachers may come into conflict with community members.

In 2019, a judge in the UK ordered an exclusion zone to remain in place around a primary school in Birmingham to prevent ongoing protests. The school was offering an LGBT (Lesbian, Gay, Bisexual and Transgendered) education programme which protesters thought inappropriate for primary school-aged children and believed conflicted with their faith, arguing that the school had a duty to consult the local community. An educational psychologist stated that she had been contacted by 21 staff members who were exhibiting symptoms of stress due to the protests (Parveen, 2019).

In this instance, we see teachers unnecessarily inserted into the middle of an essentially political question. It should not be the role of teachers to moderate conflicting demands, negotiate with local communities and decide upon curriculum content. That is a job for elected representatives.

Critical thinking or critical theory?

You meet an attractive stranger in a café. The stranger has an unusual name and you do not know their past. Mysterious and seductive, the stranger becomes your lover. Five years later, you are both in a bathroom. Your lover is taking a pee as you brush your teeth. There are no mysteries left. If you still find your lover beautiful and fulfilling – if you are still in love – then you may stay together for life. If not, you may be wondering where it all went wrong and why you have wasted so much time on this one person.

We fall for ideologies in much the same way as we fall in love. It begins when we are young. We fully commit, for a period of time at least, forsaking all others. While this may be healthy in a relationship, it is harmful in an ideology because it prevents us from exercising that tenet of critical thinking – seeing an issue from multiple perspectives. The ideologue sees the world through only one monomaniacal perspective. Others who dissent from this perspective do not hold a valid alternative view. They have been misled, are personally flawed or are, at worst, evil.

Critical theory is a perspective, originating in Marxism and filtered through academia, that has left college and now has an independent life staking out a position on one side of the ongoing culture wars of liberal democracies. Critical theory can take on a broad sense or a narrower sense and can relate to various fields of endeavour, from literary criticism to education research. Whichever way we view it, a key theme becomes apparent – critical theory views societal relationships mainly in terms of domination and oppression and seeks social transformation (Bohman, 2005).

Despite the fact that critical theory is often deployed to critique other ideologies or even the hidden ideologies we may not be aware we possess, critical theory, with its lens of emancipation from oppression through societal change, is itself a distinctive way of viewing the world – an ideology with embedded assumptions that could reasonably be challenged. Clearly, critical theory's priorities, concerns and analysis differ from those of classical liberalism, mainstream conservatism, social democracy or religious movements such as Christianity or Islam. Yet, superficially at least, critical theory presents as a set of tools for analysis and critique – a set of critical thinking tools.

In his highly influential 1968 work, *Pedagogy of the Oppressed*, first published in English in 1970, Paulo Freire applied concepts from critical theory to the field of education. The educational methods that Freire proposed are similar to nineteenth-century progressivists or more recent constructivists – traditional education he described as the 'banking model' where students are viewed as 'containers' or 'receptacles' to be filled:

> In the banking concept of education, knowledge is a gift bestowed by those who consider themselves knowledgeable upon those whom they consider to know nothing. Projecting an absolute ignorance onto others, a characteristic of the ideology of oppression, negates education and knowledge as processes of inquiry.

Why we must assume absolute ignorance on the basis of students is unclear. Could they not know a great deal already, just not the thing we are about to teach them? As we shall see in the next chapter, establishing what students already know is a key part of effective explicit teaching. Clearly, Freire sees explicit teaching as a component in the apparatus of oppression and thus takes a somewhat dim view of it. Instead, Freire presents the idea of problem-posing education, an example of which is giving peasants a photograph to consider – the parallels with current enquiry-based learning programmes are clear.

However, *Pedagogy of the Oppressed* reads mainly as a political, revolutionary, text. Throughout, Freire assumes a distinction between oppressors and the oppressed, although it is never entirely clear who belongs to each category. In more recent times, this ambiguity has been partly resolved by the development of the concept of intersectionality (Crenshaw, 1989) – the idea that we may belong to more than one class at once.

For any student of twentieth-century history, *Pedagogy of the Oppressed* ventures some alarming ideas:

> the restraints imposed by the former oppressed on their oppressors, so that the latter cannot reassume their former position, do not constitute oppression. An act is oppressive only when it prevents people from being more fully human. Accordingly, these necessary restraints do not in themselves signify that yesterday's oppressed have become today's oppressors. Acts which prevent the restoration of the oppressive regime cannot be compared with those which create and maintain it, cannot be compared with those by which a few men and women deny the majority their right to be human.

This would appear to justify, post-revolution, the establishment of a counter-revolutionary police force, a feature of twentieth-century totalitarian regimes. In order to make these connections, of course, you would need to know about this history.

In his Foreword to the abridged version of *The Gulag Archipelago*, Aleksandr Solzhenitsyn's meticulously researched epic about the Soviet Union's system of arbitrary arrest, torture, transportation and detention in remote labour camps, he warns his Western readers: 'There always is this fallacious belief: "It would not be the same here; here such things are impossible." Alas, all the evil of the twentieth century is possible everywhere on Earth.'

Whether you are a realist who believes in an objective reality that we may, in time, come to more fully apprehend, or a relativist who is sceptical about the possibility of one reality, taking instead the view that there are many prisms through which to view the world, you should be suspicious of totalising ideologies. Even if there is one truth, it seems unlikely that anyone knows it, and so those who claim to have some fully worked out system for describing the world and proposing solutions is either deluded or deceiving. If there is one principle of critical thinking we should all be able to uphold, it is to be suspicious of claims to the truth.

Therefore, teaching a perspective like critical theory, and its current manifestation in identity politics, must not be conflated with teaching critical thinking. Critical theory could well be a valuable perspective to teach in school or university, but it cannot be *the* perspective. If we teach critical theory as the only valid lens through which to view the world, we are not developing independent thinkers, but are indoctrinating young people. Teaching critical theory alongside other powerful ways of interpreting the world, such as classical liberalism, would provide students with a more rounded understanding. We should aim to teach students about ideas and not indoctrinate them into ideologies.

Dangerous magic

So, a tension has developed. Is explicit teaching such a good thing after all? If it is effective for teaching young children to read, then it may be effective for indoctrinating them into questionable ideals. Perhaps explicit teaching is dangerous magic. Yet what is the alternative? Is the problem solved by using less effective methods to teach students less well?

If we view teaching methods as distinct and independent from curriculum, then we do have to deal with an amount of moral ambiguity. Like a knife that may be used to chop onions or to stab another person, explicit teaching has no moral weight in its own right – it is just a tool that may be used for good or evil.

It is in the essentially political question of *what* we teach that moral judgements reside. Attractive as it may be for bureaucrats and politicians to dodge this question and instead appeal for the teaching of critical thinking as if it is some kind of general skill that can be applied independent of content, this is nonetheless a dodge. When those with a duty to address the question abandon this duty, it must still be addressed. And that leads to individual schools and even individual teachers shouldering this responsibility, for better or worse.

So, let us take it on. If we want our young people to develop as problem-solvers, critical thinkers and creators, then we need to identify the knowledge that will enable them to surf closest to these new understandings of the world. We cannot know for sure exactly what this knowledge is, but we can use the past to guide us and we can play the odds.

References

Bereiter, C. (2002) *Education and Mind in the Knowledge Age*. Mahwah, NJ: Lawrence Erlbaum Associates.

Bohman, J. (2005) Critical theory. *Stanford Encyclopedia of Philosophy*. Retrieved from: https://plato.stanford.edu/entries/critical-theory/

Cobb-Clark, D.A. and Schurer, S. (2012) The stability of big-five personality traits. *Economics Letters*, 115(1): 11–15.

Crenshaw, K. (1989) Demarginalizing the intersection of race and sex: A Black feminist critique of antidiscrimination doctrine, feminist theory and antiracist politics. *University of Chicago Legal Forum*, 140: 139.

Ericsson, A.K. (2008) Deliberate practice and acquisition of expert performance: A general overview. *Academic Emergency Medicine*, 15(11): 988–94.

Freire, P. (1970) *Pedagogy of the Oppressed* (trans. M.B. Ramos). New York: Continuum.

Furnham, A. and Petrides, K.V. (2003) Trait emotional intelligence and happiness. *Social Behavior and Personality: An International Journal*, 31(8): 815–23.

Graham, P. (2008, March) How to disagree. (Web essay). Retrieved from: www.paulgraham.com/disagree.html

Huber, C.R. and Kuncel, N.R. (2016) Does college teach critical thinking? A meta-analysis. *Review of Educational Research*, 86(2): 431–68.

Keynes, M. (1995) The personality of Isaac Newton. *Notes and Records of the Royal Society of London*, 49(1): 1–56.

Kirschner, P.A., Sweller, J. and Clark, R.E. (2006) Why minimal guidance during instruction does not work: An analysis of the failure of constructivist, discovery, problem-based, experiential, and inquiry-based teaching. *Educational Psychologist*, 41(2): 75–86.

Parveen, N. (2019, November) Birmingham anti-LGBT school protesters had 'misinterpreted' teachings, judge says. *The Guardian*. Retrieved from: www.theguardian.com/uk-news/2019/nov/26/birmingham-anti-lgbt-school-protests-judge-ban-permanent

Melby-Lervåg, M., Redick, T.S. and Hulme, C. (2016) Working memory training does not improve performance on measures of intelligence or other measures of "far transfer" evidence from a meta-analytic review. *Perspectives on Psychological Science*, 11(4): 512–34.

O'Keeffe, A. (2020, March) Instead of rote learning useless facts, children should be taught wellbeing. *The Guardian*. Retrieved from: www.theguardian.com/commentisfree/2020/mar/02/instead-rote-learning-useless-facts-children-need-taught-wellbeing

Ritchhart, R. and Perkins, D. (2008) Making thinking visible. *Educational Leadership*, 65(5): 57.

Sala, G. and Gobet, F. (2017) Does far transfer exist? Negative evidence from chess, music, and working memory training. *Current Directions in Psychological Science*, 26(6): 515–20.

Scott, C.L. (2015) *The Futures of Learning 3: What Kind of Pedagogies for the 21st Century?* Education Research and Foresight Working Papers. Paris: UNESCO.

Soldz, S. and Vaillant, G.E. (1999) The Big Five personality traits and the life course: A 45-year longitudinal study. *Journal of Research in Personality*, 33(2): 208–32.

Solzhenitsyn, A. (2018) *The Gulag Archipelago*. New York: Random House.

Swartz, R.J., Costa, A.L., Beyer, B.K., Reagan, R. and Kallick, B. (2010) *Thinking-Based Learning: Promoting Quality Student Achievement in the 21st Century*. New York: Teachers College Press.

Sweller, J., Ayres, P. and Kalyuga, S. (2011) Acquiring information: The borrowing and reorganising principle and the randomness as Genesis principle. In *Cognitive Load Theory*. New York: Springer, pp. 27–38.

Weitz, E., Kleiboer, A., Van Straten, A. and Cuijpers, P. (2018) The effects of psychotherapy for depression on anxiety symptoms: A meta-analysis. *Psychological Medicine*, 48(13): 2140–52.

Willingham, D.T. (2007) Critical thinking: Why it is so hard to teach? *American Federation of Teachers*, Summer, pp. 8–19.

6

HALFWAY UP A LADDER

Key Points

- We draw upon a student's prior knowledge when we teach them something new.
- Prior knowledge affects how a student will deal with new information.
- The concept of 'element interactivity' can help us understand how new information interacts with prior knowledge.
- There are a number of research-based strategies teachers may draw on in moving students from novice to expert.
- These strategies include retrieval practice, interleaving and making use of cognitive load theory effects.

Introduction

The art of explicit teaching is in deciding what to vary and when. Teaching always takes place halfway up a ladder. Contrary to the views of Paulo Freire that we met in the previous chapter, it is impossible to proceed by assuming the complete ignorance of students. Teaching in general, and explicit teaching specifically, is about using what students already know – vocabulary, ideas, analogies – to help them learn something they do not yet know. We may impose a constructivist model on this if we wish. We can talk of building schemas. But whatever the precise details of how ideas expressed by a teacher form representations in the mind of a student, the bald fact remains that the success or failure of any act of teaching is almost entirely dependent on what a student already knows.

Even at the very outset of formal education, teachers are dealing with students who can, mostly, already talk and have a modest oral vocabulary. If we view this through David Geary's model that we met in Chapter 1, we see such prior knowledge as fundamental. Academic knowledge can only ever be layered atop and co-opt the knowledge we have evolved to acquire naturally.

And yet it is no trivial matter to ascertain exactly what knowledge a student currently possesses. Knowledge is latent and we can only hope to infer its presence through the proxy of asking students questions or requesting them to complete certain tasks. Whatever human knowledge actually is, it is not like the reliable retrieval of a book from a shelf, so we can never assume that a good response to a question at a particular point in time means there will be a good response to a similar question at any later point in time. Knowledge changes and is cued by different stimuli. It's annoying like that.

Element interactivity

If it is the fate of teachers to precariously perch halfway up a ladder, then cognitive load theory gives us an insight into what this means. That insight is the concept of *element interactivity*.

We have already seen that working memory can process about four items at a time. But what is an item? In some instances, we can imagine an item being a discrete letter, whereas in others it could be the activation of an entire schema such as 'natural selection'. This, in turn, depends on what a person knows – do they possess a schema for natural selection? And so, there is an interrelationship between the processing load of working memory and the knowledge that exists in long-term memory.

It is perhaps easiest to see what is going on in the context of mathematics. Consider the following problem:

$4a = 12$

Find a

If you are a mathematics teacher, or anyone else who has studied mathematics to a sufficient level, you already know that $a = 3$. So that is one thing you had to process – you had a schema in long-term memory to do the hard work for you.

Yet what does solving this problem actually involve? First of all, there are four characters to be aware of, 4, a, = and 12. There is also a fifth character that is implied because $4a$ means $4 \times a$. However, these five items are not independent. They exist in relationship to each other. The multiplication is a relationship and the equivalence represented by the = sign is a relationship. If you move one part, it affects the others. To solve the problem, you need to know further that multiplication and division are inverse operations, so if $4 \times a = 12$, then $a = 12 \div 4$. There are a number of schemas you can build for this, and possibly the most robust is to see the equation as a balance and that if you divide one side by four to obtain a, you must divide the other side by four. So, depending on how exactly we count all of this, we are now up to about eight items. Finally, you need to know that $12 \div 4 = 3$. Hopefully, you know this as a maths fact, but if you don't, you will use additional items to work this out.

Cognitive load theory would therefore predict that any attempt to teach students how to solve such a problem from scratch would overload working memory and would fail. We can only teach such a concept from halfway up a ladder.

Part of the problem for complete novices is the large element interactivity. Not only do we have a number of elements to process but they depend on each other in specific ways, compounding the number of items to process.

In a 2017 paper, Chen et al. contrast learning to solve algebra problems with learning the chemical symbols of the periodic table.

No doubt, learning all of these symbols would be challenging. However, the element interactivity is low. Each symbol is independent of any other and could be processed in working memory alone.

Importantly, element interactivity is not a property of the task alone (see Figure 6.1). At the same time as being high in element interactivity for novices, for a relative expert, $4a = 12$ is a low element interactivity task because the expert already has schemas constructed to deal with it and so can deploy these schemas with relatively little effort. This may account for the *expertise reversal effect* we met in Chapter 3 in which relative experts learn more from solving problems than studying worked examples – a reversal of the pattern for novices.

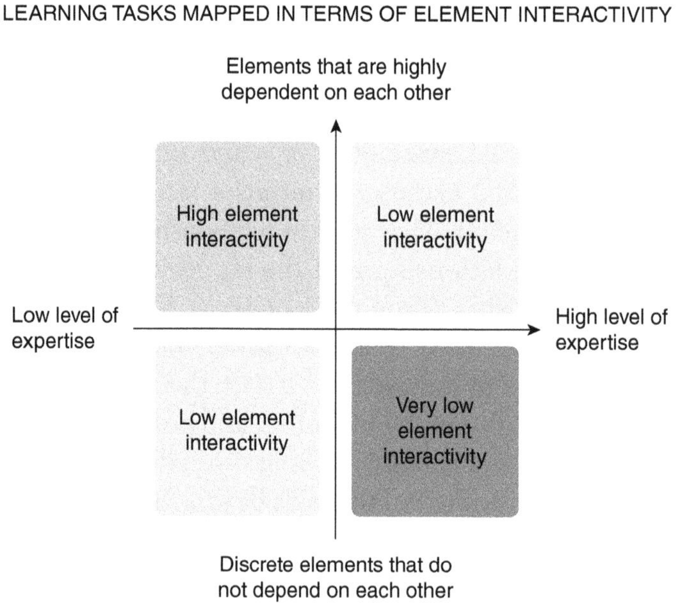

LEARNING TASKS MAPPED IN TERMS OF ELEMENT INTERACTIVITY

Elements that are highly
dependent on each other

High element
interactivity

Low element
interactivity

Low level of
expertise

High level of
expertise

Low element
interactivity

Very low
element
interactivity

Discrete elements that do
not depend on each other

Figure 6.1 Element interactivity depends on task complexity and level of expertise

Element interactivity is a controversial concept in the research literature, sometimes because people have misunderstood it to be solely a property of the task, with no reference to the level of expertise of the subject. However, where it has been better understood, the concept has been challenged on two main grounds. First, it is impossible to precisely enumerate the elements involved in many common teaching situations, so the concept is less meaningful if it is difficult for different researchers to measure. Second, experimental studies have not generally varied the level of element interactivity within a single experimental design, so conclusions about the effect of element interactivity on learning are necessarily weak (Karpicke and Aue, 2015)

This final criticism has started to be addressed by researchers investigating the *element-interactivity effect* (see e.g. Chen et al., 2015) and was part motivation for my PhD research work (Ashman et al., 2020). My research consisted of a series of experiments in which middle-school science students were given data on different light globes and were asked to decide which was the most 'energy saving'. The students were randomised into two groups. In the first group, students were asked to come up with their own solution to the problem, while the other group completed an unrelated reading filler task. Next, all students were given interactive explicit teaching together on how to solve the problem by calculating efficiency. Finally, the group that had started with problem-solving completed the reading task and the other group completed the problem-solving task. In their next science lesson, students completed a post-test which had two components – a set of questions identical to those in the problem-solving booklet but with different numbers and a set of 'transfer' questions where aspects of the questions were changed, such as replacing light globes with electric fans or adding redundant information.

This pitted the predictions of cognitive load theory – that students would learn more by explicit teaching followed by problem-solving – against the predictions of a theory known as 'productive failure' (Kapur, 2016) – that students should learn more from problem-solving prior to explicit teaching. The latter draws on the idea that there is something positive about struggle – it prepares you better for learning. There have been studies published demonstrating empirical support for productive failure (e.g. Kapur, 2014), although in the paper I co-authored, we question their design.

In both of my published experiments, element interactivity was relatively high, but in one experiment, it was made even higher by requiring students to complete an additional step. In the slightly lower element interactivity condition, explicit teaching first was superior for the identical questions, but there was no real difference on the transfer questions. When element interactivity was increased, explicit teaching first was superior for both sets of questions.

Thinking hard

The practical relevance of this research is that we should be cautious about applying approaches such as productive failure. There is a large body of research that shows the benefits of introducing supposedly desirable difficulties into learning. It is, perhaps, common sense to conclude that we learn more when we have to think hard. It may be common sense, but as a blanket statement, it is false. Thinking hard is good, right up to the point where it becomes bad.

The deliberate introduction of difficulties seems to be beneficial when element interactivity is low and so cognitive load is low (Ashman et al., 2020). For instance, if you wanted students to memorise a list of the capital cities of each state and territory in Australia, then that may be a challenging task, but it is necessarily low in element interactivity, even for novices. Assuming some facility with English, we are only asking them to process one item at a time. So, you could perhaps give them the first letter, ask them to guess, correct them and repeat the process. Such a task is structurally similar to the kinds of task that reliably show a *generation effect* in the research literature (see, for example, Hirshman and Bjork, 1988; De Winstanley and Bjork, 2004; McCurdy et al., 2020). However, due to element interactivity also decreasing as a result of greater expertise, we should also consider introducing desirable difficulties later in a sequence of instruction. Exactly what this looks like will depend on where we are on the ladder.

In mathematics, we may begin by initially presenting pared-back examples that contain only the information relevant to a question before asking students to follow these steps to solve a near-identical problem. As expertise grows, there are a number of different strategies we could apply. We may, for instance, choose to add extraneous information or embed the problem in a worded question or a (pseudo) real-world application. At some point, we may choose to present a variety of different problem types set in the same context so that students also have to determine which kind of problem each is. Alternatively, we may present problems with the same solution methods but set in different contexts. Eventually, we would want to simply present a wide variety of problems so that students have to retrieve the solution methods. These are all types of variation we could potentially introduce and we will see what the evidence tells us about them.

Reflecting on what I now understand about the sequencing of instruction, I realise that the default explicit teaching strategies that I used early in my career increased the difficulty level at too high a rate. I would present an example and then ask students to immediately solve a slightly different problem because I didn't see the point in asking them to solve an identical one. I would also present a string of different examples before setting an exercise that contained this variety of examples. Both strategies likely overloaded a proportion of students in my class.

Maths is a useful exemplar for considering a learning pathway because it is so self-contained. Other subjects are leakier. What do we need to consider when designing a pathway for English or history? Liberal arts subjects have an interplay between content and skills. In the case of English, this has often led to a focus on the skills of reading and writing as well as the features of different genres, and in the case of history, there is an awkwardness about whether we are teaching history content knowledge, skills such as composing a paragraph – a high element interactivity task for novices – or skills such as source analysis.

The problem of multiple, competing objectives can be conveniently if unsatisfactorily resolved by focusing on activities to be completed rather than what we want students to learn, and so a lot of activity-based planning occurs. Students are assigned essays to write, don't do a great job and then teachers undertake penance by staying up to the small hours writing a commentary on each essay explaining a small sample of the things that are wrong with it. It should occur to us that it may be better to teach students how to do it right in the first place.

What would that look like? If your focus is on content, then you can reduce the overall load by dialling down the writing demands. If your focus is on writing, then you can dial down the content. It will be easier for students to write well-formed sentences about a day-trip to the beach than about the consequences of the French Revolution for French society.

And this leads to a problem with assessment. If we assume that there is such a thing as a general ability to write persuasively, and that we can measure and score this ability, then we may be mystified when such scores bob up and down as we vary the context. Writing about hard things is harder than writing about easy things. A perfect score on an essay about why we should abolish school uniform does not imply that a student will gain a perfect score on an essay arguing that the origins of the First World War are best understood in terms of Thucydides' theory of hegemonic conflict.

Writing should therefore proceed through a series of ever more demanding contexts and, at each new step, we should expect some degradation of writing performance as more student attention has to be devoted to the concepts. Such a sequence is not encouraged by a system of high-stakes standardised testing that requires students to write about utterly banal topics every year or so. In such education systems, it is the role of teachers to keep an eye on the long game.

To contain cognitive load, we could decouple competing objectives as much as possible early in the learning process. For instance, if the aim of a High School English unit is for students to write about George Orwell's *1984*, then a good start may be determining whether they had read it and understood the key ideas – an initial focus on content. Rather than trying to establish this through a complex written task, a multiple-choice or fill-in-the-gaps task would allow students to focus only on those ideas.

We have already met *The Writing Revolution* (Hochman and Wexler, 2017), a sequence developed by Judith Hochman and colleagues that offers a structured approach to teaching writing. Interestingly, its focus is on learning content through writing and the approach offers a number of strategies that exist at the sentence level, such as sentence expansion, that students use when interacting with new content. Once routine, such strategies require little effort over and above the effort of dealing with new content and they embed useful writing structures that students may then draw on when writing more extended pieces. However, *The Writing Revolution* is not just about sentences; it is a bottom-up system that proceeds along a pathway from simple to complex and, as such, represents a good model of explicit writing/content instruction for those trying to wean themselves off the activity-based approach.

Ultimately, sequences of instruction are complicated constructions. Every meeting of my mathematics department is about refining them, trading off competing demands and looking for evidence from student work that can help us become more effective. That's how we established the model of slow-motion problems I described in Chapter 3. Developing such a sequence is about deciding what and when to vary, decisions that must be informed by assessment.

Cognitive load theory effects

Cognitive load theory has established a number of 'effects' that work by optimising cognitive load and managing element interactivity (see Sweller et al., 2019 for a full discussion). Whether you accept the assumptions of cognitive load theory or not, the effects are based on a large number of experiments. The effects will likely remain, even if they end up part of an enhanced or altered theory. What follows is not a comprehensive survey of all cognitive load theory effects, but it does describe a number that are relevant to planning teaching sequences.

The first effect to be established was the *goal-free effect.* One of the difficulties with asking novices to solve problems is that they tend to use a natural problem-solving strategy known as means–ends analysis. This involves comparing the current problem state with the goal state and deciding which move will take them closer to the goal state. Such a process generates a large amount of cognitive load because of the need to hold the goal state, the current state and the relationship between the two in mind. Instead, if we avoid asking for a specific result but instead ask students to work out whatever they can about a problem situation, the load is reduced because the goal state and its relationship to the current state are no longer items to be attended to, so more working memory is available for schema building. This works particularly well for certain kinds of mathematics problems. Consider Figure 6.2. Traditionally, we may ask students to find the value of angle β. However, a goal-free version of this problem may be to ask students to 'Find out whatever you can' about the situation.

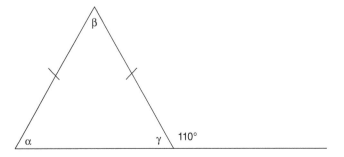

Figure 6.2 A mathematical problem that could be used for a goal-free task

The next effect to be established was one we have already met, the *worked-example effect.* This is perhaps more widely applicable than the goal-free effect and it arises from experimental studies that show novices learn more by studying worked examples than by problem-solving. However, not all ways of using worked examples are equal. For instance, researchers have found that presenting a worked example and asking subjects to immediately solve a similar problem is superior to presenting a number of different worked examples before asking subjects to solve a series of similar problems – i.e. worked examples are better presented in 'example-problem pairs' (Sweller et al., 2011). This effect may be due to the need to complete a similar problem, increasing subjects' attention to the example.

Similarly, the *completion problem effect* forces attention to the worked example. For instance, when computer science students are simply given a program to study, they are likely to pay less attention than if presented with a program with a few steps missing that they have to work out. Logically, finding the solution to the missing steps has to be something already within the subject's capability, otherwise this will generate a substantial load from a means–ends analysis search. It is therefore perhaps a bridging strategy or a strategy to be used when the worked examples in question are complex, as is the case with computer programs. An alternative that may also work by requiring students to attend to a worked example is the *self-explanation effect*, where students learn more from worked examples when provided with prompts asking them to explain to themselves what is happening.

The *split-attention effect* arises out of an apparent failure of the worked-example effect. Imagine presenting students with a worked example in the form of a diagram. However, in this diagram the different elements are labelled A, B, C and so on, and there is a key at the side of the diagram where students look up what these labels refer to. Empirical research suggests that splitting attention in this way between the diagram and the key creates unnecessary cognitive load and that placing the full labels directly on to the appropriate area of the diagram is superior.

The *redundancy effect* arises when the same, complete set of information is presented simultaneously in two different ways. This produces unnecessary cognitive load as the student does not necessarily know that the two sources are the same and has to decide what to attend to. It is perhaps easiest to understand this with the example of a diagram that fully demonstrates a particular process presented alongside text that also details the same process. However, the redundancy effect potentially arises *whenever* there are two sources of the same information presented at the same time. For instance, presenting a slide containing text while simultaneously paraphrasing that text – a common teaching practice – would be likely to induce the redundancy effect.

Conversely, information from different sources can be complementary if neither source represents a complete set of information and if the sources represent different modalities – i.e. one is visual and the other auditory. This is known as the *modality effect*. It arises because it is thought that visual and auditory information are processed independently in working memory and so, by providing a source of each, we can partially circumvent the usual working memory constraints. For instance, if we were able to remove the visual labels on a diagram entirely and replace them with an auditory commentary, that may be even more effective than having the labels integrated on the diagram.

However, with auditory information, we need to be aware of the *transient information effect*. If students need to hold on to auditory information for a period of time after it has been presented, then that will consume considerable cognitive load. Written text does not suffer from this issue, but other work-arounds include presenting auditory information in the form of a recording that can be paused and rewound.

The *variability effect* describes the finding that when cognitive load is relatively low, such as when studying worked examples, a certain amount of variability in problem types leads to better transfer of learning. This is similar to the idea of interleaving that we will encounter below and is a key question in instructional design. For novices, being presented with similar-looking problems that require different solution methods can help them to distinguish the defining features that imply a particular method. However, relative experts can already make these distinctions and so they may be better suited to practising solving similar problems in a range of different contexts (Scheiter and Gerjets, 2007).

We have already met the expertise reversal effect where, contrary to the result for relative novices, relative experts tend to learn more from problem-solving than studying worked examples. This *overarching effect* gives us a pointer to how and why we may vary instruction as a teaching sequence progresses. In essence, the expertise reversal effect, the element interactivity effect that we met above, and the *guidance-fading effect*, where students benefit from the gradual fading of levels of guidance as a course progresses, are likely to all be aspects of the same phenomenon, even though the effects are derived from different experiments. As students gain relative expertise within a particular domain of study, we need to vary the instruction, shifting from a guided approach centred on worked examples to a less-guided approach where students work more independently.

With all of these effects, it is worth trying to hold on to *why* they work. I am not aware of any *don't-put-a-funny-gif-next-to-key-information effect*, but cognitive load theory would predict that a funny gif would consume working memory resources, leaving less for the key information. There is nothing wrong with adding a little humour to your class, but separate it in time from a critical concept you want students grasp.

Asking lots of questions

The most basic variation a teacher can make to an instructional sequence is a reversal of the initial process of instruction. Instead of attempting to communicate something to a student, we ask the student to communicate something back to us, a peer or even themselves through self-assessment.

The first mistake we may make is to see these two processes – from teacher to student and from student to teacher – as completely separate phases. Rosenshine's Principles of Instruction (2012) rightly call on teachers to ask lots of questions and constantly check for understanding. It may still be necessary in some university courses for students to attend a series of lectures and then complete an exam, but it is neither necessary nor desirable in a classroom. We should ask, ask and ask again as part of the learning process, and use the results of these assessments to reteach as necessary or refine our next steps.

An excellent resource for different 'formative assessment' strategies is Dylan Wiliam's *Embedded Formative Assessment* (2017). It seems that Wiliam has been fighting a battle over many years to convince us that formative assessment is a *process* that informs teaching and not an object. A 'formative assessment' is not a sheet of paper that looks like a test and that we are going to ask students to complete on

Tuesday of next week. Whether such a test operates formatively or not depends on what we then do with it. We may well use the results to inform our next teaching steps, but we could just as well use the feedback we receive from asking an oral question in class in the same way.

One key principle of formative assessment is the need to collect evidence from *all* of our students. It would be weird for a teacher to turn up to class, wave a test and ask, 'Now, can I have a volunteer to complete this?' When we give tests, we give them to the whole class. The trouble is that if we then find out that half of the class have learnt little from the last six weeks of teaching, then that's a bit too late.

And yet we often allow only volunteers to answer questions in class. This may be because the teacher only selects students who have their hands raised, or because students simply call out answers. If it is the latter, then some work needs to be done on classroom management (see Ashman (2018) for a discussion on how to improve classroom management).

Instead of relying on volunteers, we should do one of two things. The first option is to sample from the students by setting up routines where the teacher decides which student is to answer each question. The teacher then needs a mechanism for ensuring that, over time, all students are called upon. Such a mechanism could be truly random – by drawing names printed on laminated cards out of a cup or using an electronic randomiser – or at the discretion of the teacher. However, teacher discretion needs to be self-monitored closely to ensure that some students do not get left out – I often use a version of the class list which I annotate every time I ask a question.

An alternative option is to require an answer from the entire class. This is now my favoured mechanism. All my students have mini whiteboards and we have developed a routine for their use. When I ask a question, I can see a response from the entire class, just like a test, only I now have the ability to do something about any misunderstandings.

I am often told that mini whiteboards may work well in mathematics but are completely unsuitable for subject X because subject X is so much more subjective and sophisticated than maths. This may be true. Only a subject expert could fully address that point. However, I am aware of mini whiteboards being used successfully in a wide range of subjects and if you think they could not be used successfully in yours, then I would ask you to consider one question:

'Have you broken down your initial teaching into small enough steps?' Systems that call upon all students to respond, not just volunteers, have another, more basic, advantage. If students know they might be asked a question at any time, they may pay more attention in class.

Nonetheless, the different forms of student assessment can generate a great deal of heat in schools. A couple of times in my career, I have taught a student who has a specific issue that means that it would be inappropriate to call on them in class – whatever rule you have in a school, there are always exceptions. However, there are those who will object to questioning students in this way by appealing to the notion that it is a general cause of stress for all students. I do not accept that. In a positive and respectful classroom culture where mistakes do not result in sarcasm from the teacher or mockery from peers, questioning is a perfectly normal process that should not cause anyone to feel undue pressure.

Another problem arises from the conflation of formative assessment with summative assessment. Formative assessment is often seen as cuddlier than mean old summative assessment due to the role that summative assessment plays in grading and sorting students, and the impact it often has on subsequent academic and career pathways.

However, I don't simply wish to assert the distinction between formative and summative assessment and leave it there; I would like to point out that summative assessment has been unfairly maligned. Those who seek to abolish exams often do so on the basis that they should be replaced with a more humane system that recognises the sum of a student's achievements rather than their performance on a single day.

Yet exams exist for a reason. No, they are never going to be a completely level playing field. Some students have tutors. Some receive inadequate teaching. If your father is a physics teacher, you probably have an advantage on the physics exam. Nevertheless, when a student goes into an exam room, they cannot take a tutor with them – they are on their own. The work they produce over that couple of hours has to be theirs.

Any alternative to exams is a far less level playing field. What about a portfolio assessment? Tutors can have far more influence over a portfolio assessment than an exam. Or perhaps we decide to factor in non-cognitive abilities and reward those who do community service. What could be wrong with that? Community service is a good thing, right? Well, the student who lives at home with a single parent, works at weekends and takes three buses to school is going to find it much harder to find the time and opportunity for community work than the affluent kid with connections at the local church. How about assessment based on real-world projects or work experience? Well, imagine comparing the engineering project of the student whose uncle is a professor of engineering with that of his peers. Exams have been maligned, but perhaps they represent the least bad system for providing a measure of performance that universities and employers can reliably use.

Retrieval practice

Asking students questions – or students asking themselves questions through the use of, for example, flashcards – has developed the fancy name of 'retrieval practice'. You may see that some refer to it as the *testing effect*, but those people didn't get the memo that the word 'testing' sounds mean and frightening.

Of all learning strategies, retrieval practice probably has the soundest evidence base (Karpicke and Grimaldi, 2012). It works. The more we ask students to recall stuff, the easier it becomes to recall, although I would add the proviso that the stuff has to be in there first.

Teachers sometimes play the game of 'guess what's in my head?'. Instead of teaching something and then asking students to retrieve it, teachers try to lead students to a new understanding they have not yet taught them by asking a series of questions. You know the sort of thing:

Teacher: Jake, why do satellites stay in orbit?

Jake: I dunno, rockets?

Teacher: Rockets need fuel, lots of it. So where do satellites store that?

Jake: In fuel tanks?

Teacher: They don't have the room. The tanks would be too big. So, how do you think they stay in orbit?

Jake: They get refuelled?

Teacher: What if they don't use rockets at all?

Jake: But they do, don't they? You see them launch on rockets.

Teacher: But what if that's just to get into space? How do they then *stay* in space?

And so on until, presumably, Jake figures out his own version of Newtonian mechanics. Frustrating exchanges of this kind must be based on the folk theory that figuring something out for yourself is somehow superior to having it explained to you. However, any such folk theory appears to be false. As we saw with the generation effect, for some low element interactivity objectives, adding an element of discovery in this way may be helpful, and an element of fill-in-the-gaps may aid learning from larger worked examples, as in the completion problem effect, but there is little value in asking students to try to figure out complex concepts for themselves.

So, we need to actually teach Jake about satellite motion before we start asking him questions. At this point, retrieval becomes a powerful tool. The questioning should start straight away after we have taught the concept – in the same class – and also continue, way into the future when we are teaching a different topic entirely. That's because there is evidence that spaced practice has benefits for learning (see, for example, Donovan and Radosevich, 1999). By constantly having to retrieve concepts over an extended period of time, we seem to train the mind that these concepts are important. Bjork and Bjork's 'new theory of disuse' (1992) suggests that concepts have both a retrieval and a storage strength. Some are stored in the mind very strongly but are hard to recover. For example, a phone number you had ten years ago is probably still stored but is hard to retrieve. In contrast, while you are staying in a hotel, you can easily retrieve your room number, but that number is unlikely to have high storage strength. A week later and it is effectively – if not literally – gone. Performance at any given time depends on retrieval strength.

The New Theory of Disuse proposes that there is no effective limit on storage in long-term memory but there are limits on retrieval. Moreover, when we retrieve something, we add to both its storage and retrieval strength. These gains are greater when it is harder to retrieve and this may explain why spaced practice, which makes it harder to retrieve an item, is effective.

The same effect may be behind another variation we can layer in to learning. In interleaving, instead of students practising a block of problems of type A, a block of problems of type B and then a block of problems of type C, all three problem types are randomly mixed so that a student may, for instance, complete the sequence ABACBACABC. When compared to blocked practice, interleaving shows learning gains. This may be because it distributes the problems over a long time period – in other words, *a spaced practice effect* – or it may be because it helps students to learn the similarities and differences between problems in the same domain (Foster et al., 2019) – an effect similar to cognitive load theory's variation effect.

Learning the similarities and differences between problem types is no trivial matter (Willingham, 2002). As we saw in Chapter 3, novices tend to be drawn to the surface features of problems and the process of developing expertise is linked to an appreciation of the underlying structure.

Returning to the thought experiment of teaching logical fallacies that we met in Chapter 5, we should predict that, initially at least, students would be able to correctly identify a logical fallacy in one context but not in a different one. They may, for instance, realise that 'you're an idiot!' is an *ad hominem*, but fail to recognise that 'your argument is typical of the metropolitan liberal elite' is also an *ad hominem*. This is another example of the hard problem of transfer of learning.

One way we could attempt to directly teach underlying structure is to explicitly highlight it by perhaps presenting two problems with the same deep structure but different surface features side-by-side and talking through these features. Alternatively, we could present two problems with similar surface features but a different deep structure.

What did you learn today?

My daughter often comes home from school and exclaims that she has learnt nothing that day – that her teachers were asking her to do the same old stuff that she already knows how to do. I explain to her that for some critical concepts, we don't want students to learn them until they can get them right; we want them to learn them until they cannot get them wrong. Examples may include capitalising the starts of sentences or knowing that 7 × 8 = 56. The kinds of problems and tasks that these mini problems are embedded within are complex enough to require all of a person's attention. Because of reactions such as that of my daughter, this can be a hard sell, and we often fall short of it. It is one reason why spaced practice feels counterintuitive. It feels as though we may be wasting our time doing something we can already do instead of learning something new.

Rosenshine (2012) advises obtaining a high success rate with questions asked in class and he even suggests a specific benchmark of 80 per cent. This is not completely arbitrary. It is based upon process–product research and draws on the concept of 'mastery learning' developed by Benjamin Bloom.

Initially, this feels like an odd directive. How is the success rate something the teacher can control? If students find a task hard, then that is intrinsic to whatever you are teaching. Yet recall the example of slow-motion problems. When I presented my students with a two- or three-step problem to solve, I would often not obtain a success rate of 80 per cent. But this is a sign to back up and break the task down into smaller parts. We can follow this approach all the way back down the ladder to the point where students *can* achieve such a success rate. At close to the bottom, we can say things like 'Pick up your marker, draw a circle on your mini whiteboard, then hold this up for me to check.'

As a young science teacher, I remember being amazed by a more experienced colleague who would teach science practical skills in this way. She would say things like 'I want you to pick up your test tube and place it in a rack and then put that in front of you to your right. Let's see. Josh – that's your left. Good. Now, I want you to pick up the spatula.' It blew my mind because I was asking my own students to conduct entire investigations in an atmosphere bordering on chaos. What's more, her students looked as if they were enjoying themselves, whereas mine seemed distracted.

When we first explicitly teach something, we are in control of the success rate due to the moves we decide to make. If students are finding it too hard, we can be more explicit. If it is too easy, we can introduce difficulties and variations. We have a foot on the gas.

However, we should view initial teaching of this kind as only the first stage. We need to return again and again to the same key concepts and every time we do, we will again need to adjust the level of difficulty. We should find it becomes easier with each return and so we can gradually dial up the difficulty. Students need to be taught why we are doing this – that they did not learn it the first time; they only started to learn it and the learning process needs to continue.

The reverse of the complaint that 'I didn't learn anything new today' is perhaps that, 'I've forgotten everything I learned about that.' As a maths teacher, people often feel compelled to tell me they have forgotten everything they were ever taught about algebra. And yet such a statement is probably not true. The new theory of disuse would see this algebra knowledge as being still present, with a high storage strength. What is lacking is retrieval strength as the mind deploys these limited resources elsewhere. If you were to reteach algebra to such people, provided they learnt it in the first place, you could probably progress up the ladder fairly quickly.

The effect of retrieval practice on retrieval strength is perhaps why there is evidence for the effectiveness of successive relearning – multiple spaced sessions of retrieval practice until mastery is achieved in each (Janes et al., 2019).

Skipping rungs

The curse of knowledge may cause us to try to accelerate up the ladder too soon and then not return to the concepts in question. What's more, the Dunning–Kruger effect means that students may not be able to alert us to the problem. In fact, it is quite possible that an extremely popular teacher with an affectionate nickname who students regularly give high scores on any survey of teacher quality is simultaneously hopelessly ineffective. Student ratings of teacher effectiveness show only a small to moderate correlation with students' actual achievement (Uttl et al., 2017). In one famous 1970s experiment, an actor was given essentially nonsense lines to read out, but medical students were told that he was an expert named 'Doctor Fox' (Naftulin et al., 1973). When instructed to be expressive, his acting skill was enough to convince the students to rate him highly. Teaching-as-a-popularity-contest is quite a different game from the pursuit of teacher effectiveness.

In my experience, many people are playing the teaching-as-a-popularity-contest game. They seek validation and sometimes emotional support from students. They hide in subject areas that are not rigorously assessed or they work in schools where keeping parents happy is the number one priority, with student achievement being way down the list. In many cases, they adopt rationalisations for why student achievement does not matter, arguing against standardised testing, graduation exams or rankings on the basis that these are out-dated or stressful for students. They may claim that teaching is all about relationships and that students mainly remember what kind of a person the teacher was and what they stood for, not what they taught. Or they may suggest that, in some largely undefined way, their less effective approach to teaching better prepares students for the future. What kind of monster wants to spoon-feed (i.e. teach) students? Instead, the priority must be for students to become inde-pendent learners (i.e. let the teacher off the hook for not teaching them anything).

And we can see that strategies such as successive relearning are not always going to be popular with students. If we break things down enough, our students might not even notice the progress they are making and neither might we. So, in these circumstances, it is worth making such progress explicit. If you can show a student and their parents, and yourself, a piece of writing now and a piece of writing from the start of the year, perceptions of progress can be influenced by reality.

You need to ask yourself what kind of teacher you are. Doing the right thing is not always easy and there are temptations that lead us away from this path.

References

Ashman, G. (2018) *The Truth about Teaching: An Evidence-informed Guide for New Teachers*. London: Sage.

Ashman, G., Kalyuga, S. and Sweller, J. (2020) Problem-solving or explicit instruction: which should go first when element interactivity is high? *Educational Psychology Review*, 32(1): 229–47.

Bjork, R.A. and Bjork, E.L. (1992) A new theory of disuse and an old theory of stimulus fluctuation. In Healy, A., Kosslyn, S. and Shiffrin, R. (eds), *From Learning Processes to Cognitive Processes: Essays in Honor of William K. Estes*, Vol. 2. Hillsdale, NJ: Erlbaum, pp. 35–67.

Chen, O., Kalyuga, S. and Sweller, J. (2015) The worked example effect, the generation effect, and element interactivity. *Journal of Educational Psychology*, 107(3): 689.

Chen, O., Kalyuga, S. and Sweller, J. (2017) The expertise reversal effect is a variant of the more general element interactivity effect. *Educational Psychology Review*, 29(2): 393–405.

De Winstanley, P.A. and Bjork, E.L. (2004) Processing strategies and the generation effect: Implications for making a better reader. *Memory & Cognition*, 32(6): 945–55.

Donovan, J.J. and Radosevich, D.J. (1999) A meta-analytic review of the distribution of practice effect: Now you see it, now you don't. *Journal of Applied Psychology*, 84(5): 795.

Foster, N.L., Mueller, M.L., Was, C., Rawson, K.A. and Dunlosky, J. (2019) Why does interleaving improve math learning? The contributions of discriminative contrast and distributed practice. *Memory & Cognition*, 47(6): 1088–101.

Hirshman, E. and Bjork, R.A. (1988) The generation effect: Support for a two-factor theory. *Journal of Experimental Psychology: Learning, Memory, and Cognition*, 14(3): 484.

Hochman, J.C. and Wexler, N. (2017) *The Writing Revolution: A Guide to Advancing Thinking Through Writing in All Subjects and Grades*. San Francisco, CA: Jossey Bass.

Janes, J.L., Dunlosky, J., Rawson, K.A. and Jasnow, A. (2019) Successive relearning improves performance on a high-stakes exam in a difficult biopsychology course. *Applied Cognitive Psychology*.

Kapur, M. (2014) Productive failure in learning math. *Cognitive Science*, 38(5): 1008–22.

Kapur, M. (2016) Examining productive failure, productive success, unproductive failure, and unproductive success in learning. *Educational Psychologist*, 51(2): 289–99.

Karpicke, J.D. and Grimaldi, P.J. (2012) Retrieval-based learning: A perspective for enhancing meaningful learning. *Educational Psychology Review*, 24(3): 401–18.

Karpicke, J.D. and Aue, W.R. (2015) The testing effect is alive and well with complex materials. *Educational Psychology Review*, 27(2): 317–26.

McCurdy, M.P., Sklenar, A.M., Frankenstein, A.N. and Leshikar, E.D. (2020) Fewer generation constraints increase the generation effect for item and source memory through enhanced relational processing. *Memory*, 28(5): 598–616.

Naftulin, D.H., Ware, J.E., Jr and Donnelly, F.A. (1973) The Doctor Fox lecture: A paradigm of educational seduction. *Journal of Medical Education*, 48(7): 630–35.

Rosenshine, B. (2012) Principles of Instruction: Research-based strategies that all teachers should know. *American Educator*, 36(1): 12.

Scheiter, K. and Gerjets, P. (2007) Making your own order: Order effects in system- and user-controlled settings for learning and problem solving.

In Ritter, F.E., Nerb, J., Lehtinen, E. and Oshea, T. (eds), *In Order to Learn: How the Sequence of Topics Influences Learning*. New York: Oxford University Press, pp. 195–212.

Sweller, J., Ayres, P. and Kalyuga, S. (2011) The worked example and problem completion effects. In *Cognitive Load Theory*. New York: Springer, pp. 99–109.

Sweller, J., van Merriënboer, J.J. and Paas, F. (2019) Cognitive architecture and instructional design: 20 years later. *Educational Psychology Review*, 1–32.

Uttl, B., White, C.A. and Gonzalez, D.W. (2017) Meta-analysis of faculty's teaching effectiveness: Student evaluation of teaching ratings and student learning are not related. *Studies in Educational Evaluation*, 54: 22–42.

Wiliam, D. (2017) *Embedded Formative Assessment* (2nd edn). Bloomington, IN: Solution Tree Press.

Willingham, D.T. (2002) Ask the cognitive scientist inflexible knowledge: The first step to expertise. *American Educator*, 26(4): 31–3.

7

THE GIANT SHRUGS

Key Points

- Using explicit teaching can be difficult in contexts that are hostile to it.
- Teachers can make use of their autonomy, their connections with colleagues and the wider teaching community to help navigate this challenge.

Introduction

So, what kind of teacher are you? There are those who would argue that everything I have presented in this book represents a false choice – that all teachers use explicit teaching and there is no conflict between explicit teaching and enquiry learning. But there is.

Less explicit teaching methods for early reading instruction, such as balanced literacy, are promoted by education academics in Australia (Ashman, 2018), part of a wider international effort to delegitimise explicit, systematic phonics teaching (see, for example, Davis, 2013; Brooks, 2017; National Education Policy Center, 2020). This is despite reports commissioned by the governments of English-speaking countries detailing the evidence for the effectiveness of an explicit and systematic approach (Ehri et al., 2001; Rose, 2006; Rowe, 2006). Even if there were a commitment across the system to explicit phonics teaching, there is evidence that teachers may lack sufficient knowledge (e.g. Stark et al., 2016).

Professor Pamela Snow of Latrobe University in Australia notes that, astonishingly, university undergraduates are frequently unable to write in sentences, largely because they don't appear to know what a sentence is (Snow, 2020). These undergraduates are teacher education students, so it is hard to see how to break the cycle. Jo Boaler, Professor of Maths Education at Stanford University, pours cold water on the need for students to learn multiplication facts (Ward, 2015). The reading wars rage, largely unresolved, alongside the maths wars, the enquiry learning wagon rolls across subjects from history to science, writing is often still taught through immersion and pundits regularly appear and ask why it is necessary to teach children facts, each time as if they are the first to think of such a question. New justifications are found for old ideas and the wheel turns.

You may not care for the venom spat from either side of the argument, but sides do exist. You either believe that teaching is about conveying specific concepts about the world and that the process of explicit teaching is the most effective way to do this or you believe something else. That's not a false choice.

When the giant shrugs and young people fall from his shoulders, what are we to do? If we are fortunate and work with like-minded colleagues, then we can invest our effort in collaborative curriculum development – refining the strategies and sequencing of explicit programmes. If we wish, we can decide to teach our students how to write in sentences and then we can work out the best approaches for doing this.

And yet many teachers who would like to teach explicitly face obstruction from school leaders, bureaucrats and colleagues who may have different ideas and who may even be openly hostile, falsely characterising explicit teaching as dull or, worse still, oppressive. Even those who work in a team with common aims and agreements may feel stranded in a wider community that is hostile to their aims and methods. What can we do?

The classroom door

Often, our greatest flaws also represent our greatest opportunities. One flaw in the common model of how schools are organised is that teachers have an extreme level of autonomy. When a surgeon conducts an operation, they must follow agreed protocols and there are fellow trained professionals in the operating theatre alongside the surgeon. When a teacher closes the classroom door, they are usually on their own and can do pretty much what they like.

This is a flaw because it militates against the development of commonly understood effective practices. Teachers tend to work things out for themselves, on the job, and the solutions they develop are not necessarily optimal ones. It explains why big, top-down efforts at reform, even those with a strong rationale, often fail to deliver at scale. Teachers effectively ignore them or change them out of all recognition. They do this because they can.

Yes, teachers can be observed teaching and data is often analysed to some degree, but, even when valid, most schools do not know what to do with such evidence and lack the organisational means to impose a consistent approach across all of their teachers. School leadership is rarely about managing the complex details of implementing a well-thought through plan but about introducing – but rarely fully implementing – a funky-sounding initiative that may be mentioned on a future resume.

And that's why the classroom door is also an opportunity. It's not as if all the ideas that school leaders and bureaucrats introduce are good ideas. The chances are that most of them are pretty flawed.

Bad ideas are constantly reborn in the initiative churn of schools as ambitious people seek flags to wave. And so the classroom door may also act as a shield, protecting teachers and their students from a tyranny of ineptitude.

If you are keeping your head down and your classroom door closed, waiting for this, too, to pass, you don't want to draw attention to yourself. Better to smile and nod than draw a target on your back. But it can be a lonely business.

Colleagues

And that's why we seek fellow travellers. Do you think your colleagues could be convinced? Are they ready to move on from the bad ideas they have received in training? It can be hard to tell. Most people dislike being contradicted. They rarely say, 'Thank you for disabusing me of that misconception.' Even if you present them with strong evidence and they then change their views as a result, the fact that you challenged them may still rankle. You may become seen as difficult or awkward.

A better approach may be to find a statement you do agree with: say you agree with it and then propose adding to that statement – 'Yes, and . . . ' . This usually involves listening carefully more than it does talking. Undoubtedly, we all believe in some things that are false, but working with others to improve the situation involves finding common ground.

If you come to be seen as someone with useful ideas to add to the conversation, then you may find that colleagues start to approach you and ask your opinion or for papers to read.

The wider community

When I began teaching, the education community that I was able to interact with on a regular basis consisted only of teachers in my own school. Schools have their own distinctive cultures and politics, and this often frames discussions. It becomes less about the abstract qualities of an initiative and more about who is involved and how this affects the politics.

Now, we have the opportunity afforded by social media. We can connect with other educators on Twitter and Facebook. We can attend teachmeets and researchED conferences. This wider community is shaped by wider currents. Yes, there are issues with the standard of discussion and you do have to be careful when engaging with social media as a teacher, but these avenues represent a way of focusing on the wider ideas. If you are a teacher who feels alone in your school, starting a Twitter account, whether in your own name or, if necessary, anonymously, can provide a connection to like-minded peers.

And it is through the bottom-up efforts of many teachers, co-ordinated and refined through contact via social media that we will eventually solve the problems that plague teaching – the endless recycling of bad ideas – and be able to focus on structuring and sequencing effective explicit teaching so that the next generation may see further than we ever did. Excellence should be a concern of the future and not a property of the past.

If you see a teacher on television today, it is likely that he or she is being lauded as a hero for having gone above and beyond the call of duty. Former students may gush as presenters metaphorically pat them on the head. However, if you see a discussion of teaching methods or policy, you are likely to be presented with pundits, ideologues, union officials, academics or anyone at all, really, other than practising teachers.

One day, teachers will take back control of their profession. We will be the experts. They will want to talk to us. Let's begin that journey.

References

Ashman, G. (2018, August) Science versus slurs: The phonics debate. (Blog post). *Filling the Pail*. Retrieved from: https://gregashman.wordpress.com/2018/08/01/science-versus-slurs-the-phonics-debate/

Brooks, G. (2017, November) Teaching of synthetic phonics in Australia based on flawed evidence. (Blog post). *EduResearch Matters*. Retrieved from: www.aare.edu.au/blog/?p=2577

Davis, A. (2013) To read or not to read: Decoding synthetic phonics. *Impact*, 20: 1–38.

Ehri, L.C., Nunes, S.R., Stahl, S.A. and Willows, D.M. (2001) Systematic phonics instruction helps students learn to read: Evidence from the

National Reading Panel's meta-analysis. *Review of Educational Research*, 71(3): 393–447.

National Education Policy Center (2020) *Policy Statement on the "Science of Reading"*. Retrieved from: https://nepc.colorado.edu/sites/default/files/publications/FYI%20Ed%20Deans%20reading.pdf

Rose, J. (2006) *Independent Review of the Teaching of Early Reading*. Nottingham: DfE Publications.

Rowe, K. (2006) Teaching reading: Findings from the national inquiry. *Research Developments*, 15(15): 2.

Snow, P. (2020, June) This is not a sentence. (Blog post). *The Snow Report*. Retrieved from: http://pamelasnow.blogspot.com/2020/06/this-is-not-sentence.html

Stark, H.L., Snow, P.C., Eadie, P.A. and Goldfeld, S.R. (2016) Language and reading instruction in early years' classrooms: The knowledge and self-rated ability of Australian teachers. *Annals of Dyslexia*, 66(1): 28–54.

Ward, H. (2015) 'Disastrous' focus on memorising times tables doesn't add up, argues top Stanford maths expert. *Tes*. Retrieved from: www.tes.com/news/disastrous-focus-memorising-times-tables-doesnt-add-argues-top-stanford-maths-expert

INDEX